Higher Education Pedagogies

SRHE and Open University Press Imprint

Current titles include:

Higher Education Pedagogies

A Capabilities Approach

Melanie Walker

Society for Research into Higher Education
& Open University Press

Open University Press
McGraw-Hill Education
McGraw-Hill House
Shoppenhangers Road
Maidenhead
Berkshire
England
SL6 2QL

email: enquiries@openup.co.uk
world wide web: www.openup.co.uk

and Two Penn Plaza, New York, NY 10121–2289, USA

First published 2006

Editorial material and selection © Melanie Walker 2006

A catalogue record of this book is available from the British Library

ISBN-13: 978 0335 21321 4 (pb)   978 0335 21322 1 (hb)
ISBN-10: 0335 21321 9 (pb)   0335 21322 7 (hb)

Library of Congress Cataloging-in-Publication Data
CIP data has been applied for

Typeset by RefineCatch Limited, Bungay, Suffolk
Printed in the UK by Bell & Bain Ltd, Glasgow

In memory of Stella Clark, beloved friend
1957–2005

Contents

Acknowledgements

Many thanks to the students and the lecturers who shared their insights with me, both formally and informally, in a range of higher education settings. All of them are anonymized for reasons of confidentiality. I owe an especial intellectual debt to the members of the Capability and Education Network in the UK. They have consistently challenged my thinking and moved it forward. In particular, I would like to thank Lorella Terzi, Severine Deneulin, Flavio Comim, David Bridges, Rosie Vaughan, Michael Watts, Elspeth Page, Janet Raynor and Terry McLaughlin. Of all the Network members, however, I owe the greatest obligation to Elaine Unterhalter for her rich intelligence, so generously shared, and the warmth of her friendship. Both Elaine and Richard Bates kindly read the almost-completed manuscript and offered encouragement and helpful suggestions. The ideas worked through in this book have been discussed at a number of conferences and seminars in the UK/Europe, South Africa, Australia and the USA, in conversation and in email exchanges over the last four years. At various occasions the following people have all commented or made remarks which required me to rethink or refine aspects of my argument: Richard Bates, John Elliott, Fazal Rizvi, John Field, Pat Thomson, Terri Seddon, Gloria Dall'Alba, Alan Feldman, Lyn Yates, Judyth Sachs, Susan Hodgett, Pedro Flores-Crespo, Stephen Rowland, Garth Allen, Monica McLean, Bridget Somekh, Paula Ensor, Ursula Hoadley, Carolyn Brina, and Vivienne Bozalek. Thanks to colleagues at the University of Sheffield Greg Brooks, Bob Lingard, Gareth Parry and Sue Webb, but especially Ann-Marie Bathmaker for good ideas and stimulating conversations. Thanks also to the University of Sheffield for grants towards the costs of data collection. I would also like to thank students on the Dublin EdD who are a continuing source of inspiration for aspiring towards pedagogical accomplishments in research-led teaching, and for the great pleasure I have derived from my interactions with them. The editors at the Open University Press have been unfailingly helpful and professional in their approach; my thanks to John Skelton who originally accepted my proposal and more recently to Melanie Smith and Katharine Metzler. I want also to acknowledge two very special women in my family, Victoria and Clare Gilham, for their love and encouragement, my partner Ian Phimister, for his unfailing support, and dearest Daisy. Above all, I owe an especial debt of inspiration and friendship to Stella Clark, a beloved friend and a remarkable and gifted teacher who always reminded me through her teaching and research practices that lecturers can and do make a positive difference to student learning and capability. She was a warm and extraordinary person who died too soon on 20 March 2005 at the age of 48.

Part 1

Context

1

Framing the Context of Higher Education

We often have to explain to young people why study is useful. It's pointless telling them that it's for the sake of knowledge, if they don't care
about knowledge. Nor is there any point in telling kids that an educated
person gets through life better than an ignoramus, because they can
always point to some genius who, from their standpoint, leads a
wretched life. And so the only answer is that the exercise of knowledge
creates relationships, continuity and emotional attachments. It intro-
duces us to parents other than our biological ones. It allows us to live
longer because we don't just remember our own life but the lives of
others. It creates an unbroken thread that runs from our adolescence
(and sometimes from infancy) to the present day. And all this is very
beautiful.

(Umberto Eco, 2004: 7)

This chapter opens with a very brief and unapologetically partial selection of
lecturer and student voices as expressions of what I take to be 'educated
hope' (Giroux, 2001: 2) about higher education in order to establish at the
outset the approach of this book. I have set out to produce a narrative which
articulates a guarded optimism about higher education as a site for personal
engagement, transformation and change through individual development
and the potential contribution of higher education and its graduates to
social well-being and public life. The late Edward Said (quoted in Higgins,
2001: 22) argued as a university teacher that 'the whole idea of education is
to change and improve things, so that other cultural and political possibilities can emerge, even at moments when so-called pragmatists say this is
impossible'. Any country, he asserts, owes the well-being of its citizens not
only to the state of its economy but also to the health of its public culture and
the nurturing of lively and viable intellectual communities in and through
critical reading in higher education. We ought to learn 'to deal sceptically
and perhaps even subversively with injustice, dogmatic authority, corruption
and all the blandishments of power' (quoted in Higgins, 2001: 22). Martha

Nussbaum (2002) believes that the job of a university teacher and philosopher (and she is both) is to make human life better. She writes that becoming an educated citizen in and through higher education (and hence the purposes of her teaching) means acquiring knowledge and analytical skills but also 'learning how to be a human being capable of love and imagination' (2002: 301).

Turning now from these two university teachers to a teacher and his students in a first-year hispanic studies tutorial in Glasgow, lecturer Mike Gonzalez asks whether any of the students have questions about the book they are studying, an early novel by Garcia Marquez. One student wants to know what exam questions they might expect. Mike responds by asking the students what issues they might set themselves as essay topics and one student suggests something on 'style'. Mike continues the story:

> I wondered what they understood by style and suggested that we might go round the room and get each person to mention a book they had read and how they would describe its style. Natasha talked about Hardy's *Mayor of Casterbridge*; Emily brought up Angela Carter and her magic realism, Michelle talked about Toni Morrison's *Beloved*, Suzie described Grassic Gibbon's *Sunset Song* (which she wasn't all that impressed by), Matthew asked whether the James Bond novels had a style at all or were simply formulaic. Everyone had a book to suggest . . . This was a randomly chosen first-year tutorial group on a Tuesday afternoon. And they say students don't read anymore.
>
> (in Phipps and Gonzalez, 2004: 131–2)

Next, a student studying with Tara Brabazon (2002) in Western Australia, writes an email to her about her learning on the Cultural Difference and Diversity course, saying:

> On the whole this unit has at times been very disruptive to virtually my whole life, ...i have been forced to question myself and my assumptions and common sense notions about identity etc, more times than is reasonable in one semester. i love those units where you feel a little bit unstable at the end, and its also very good (very frustrating) when you come out of a unit with many more questions than answers. In the words of some ancient guy long passed on, the only thing i know now is that I know nothing. this is a good thing.
>
> (quoted in Brabazon, 2002: 39)

Finally, a student interviewed around 10 years ago on why he had wanted to study at the University of the Western Cape in South Africa declared hopefully, 'I longed to be here because of it being the People's University and where democracy is being practised and where the doors of learning and culture are opened' (quoted in Ruth, 1993: 22).

From here, this book takes up what ought to be a central issue in contemporary higher education – a criterion of justice for evaluating e/quality. As more and more students enter higher education and it shifts from élite to mass provision in many countries, the moral role of higher education regarding citizenship and democratic life is then foregrounded (Englund, 2002). This is no minor matter, and it is no minor matter at the present historical juncture and the problems that beset our world. In their important account of how some USA universities are preparing undergraduates for lives of moral and civic responsibility, Anne Colby and her colleagues (2003) invoke John Adams, architect of the Massachusetts constitution. Adams understood, Colby *et al.* (2003: viii) argue, that democratic society is grounded in a social compact entered into by citizens with each other and with the whole community or society. This in turn requires 'an educated citizenry blessed with virtue as well as wisdom and knowledge'. Higher education, in particular, is a period when students ought to develop the maps, tools and resources, they say, for the journeys which follow. More than this, their preparations can directly shape the course of the subsequent journey:

> Maps direct the travelers towards one set of paths rather than another. Available tools dispose explorers to seek out particular kinds of terrain. Their choice of comrades also opens up some options while foreclosing others. And the knowledge and values they acquire equip them to respond effectively to the unpredictable challenges and opportunities that will inevitably confront them in their travels.
>
> (2003: viii).

In this book, I therefore work to develop a justice criterion using Amartya Sen's (1992, 1999, 2002) capability approach to show how the approach might help take thinking forward, specifically in this book in relation to a 'thick', progressive and ethical understanding of undergraduate pedagogical practices. Here I take a progressive higher education pedagogy 'to signify a broad commitment to democratizing our lives and institutions' (Apple, 1993: 8). By ethics I also mean specifically teaching and learning action which is ethical to the extent that 'it is sympathetically informed by an understanding of its impact on the welfare and interests of those who are likely to be affected by it' (Bagnall, 2002: 79). For example, a pedagogical focus on 'leaner-centredness' which encourages students 'to make decisions on behalf of themselves and only on behalf of themselves', Bagnall (2002: 83), would in my view be counter-ethical practice. It is to underline again that higher education, as Colby *et al.* (2003: xii) argue, 'can be pivotal, leading to new ways of understanding the world and one's place in the world'. In short, higher education and what kind and form of higher education, matters.

I engage specifically with capability as a development discourse and use it to examine higher education pedagogy from this point of view. The book is the product of my own journey of understanding over the last eight years in higher education in the UK, and my attempts to find ways to talk about pedagogy as structurally and contextually located but also as a matter of micro-processes of capability development, agency and learning in which we make futures. I am concerned above all with developing a more ethical and reflexive account of higher education from an insider point of view of a researcher and a practitioner. The book does not seek to develop a comprehensive theory of higher education pedagogy or learning, nor does it pretend to offer an exhaustive set of case studies from many universities across all disciplines. Instead it sets out to provide illustrative stories of peda-gogy, to critically exemplify and illustrate the argument being made, drawing on the rich qualitative interview data from two projects in particular – 'Teaching For Critical Learning', and 'First Generation – Widening Partici-pation Students', and is informed by an earlier collaborative action research project on 'Critical Professionalism' (Walker, 2001a).

Hard times for higher education

Now, in these difficult times for higher education in all parts of the world, a perspective on higher education as fostering 'educated hope' and ethical and critical citizens, as well as economic development and economic life, seems increasingly at risk, even naive. The idea of higher education as a public good, enriching both the individual and all of society, has arguably been overtaken by a rhetoric of business models and market relations, together with an audit and accounting regulatory culture. Higher education is as a result increasingly regarded as a private commodity rather than a public good. Pessimists assert the decline or erasure of critical learning in the 'ruins' (Readings, 1996) of the university, 'except as the rear-guard protests of an exhausted faculty and a fragment of the largely demobilized student body' (Aronowitz and Giroux, 2000: 338). A language of customers, com-petition, efficiency gains and value for money, Halsey (1992) argues, has replaced older relations of trust. He notes bluntly that academics have been invited to believe that increasing student numbers relative to academic staff could be counted as an efficiency gain. To this must be added the impact of new theories of economic growth which have conferred on education, on knowledge production and the knowledge society (replacing an older indus-trial model) a central role as an essential engine of such growth. Chapters in a recent edited collection (Walker and Nixon, 2004) detail: the suppression of ethical dispositions in everyday life in universities (Zipin and Brennan, 2004); the effect on academic identities of the research assessment regime in the UK (Lucas, 2004); the neo-conservative assault on the curriculum in the USA (Selden, 2004); and, the university in crisis in the face of globalization, neoliberal policies and the knowledge economy (Peters, 2004). In their edited collection, Henry Giroux and Kostas Myriades (2001) point to cor-porate university cultures and the spread of commercial values in higher education where 'social visions are dismissed as hopelessly out of date' (Giroux, 2001: 3). In a recent book on contemporary life in British uni-versities, Mary Evans (2004) suggests in her title *Killing Thinking*, the death of universities under current regimes of funding, regulation and account-ability. After rehearsing her arguments in the book, she concludes that uni-versities are in fact unlikely to collapse, but she also suggests that they may 'empty of creative engagement and creativity, as new generations, having experienced the deadly possibilities of the bureaucratised university, refuse to consider further involvement with that world and take their energies and talents elsewhere' (2004: 152). No wonder Stephen Rowland (2001) asked in his inaugural professorial lecture, 'Is the University a place of learning?'

This is not to say that there is an international consensus about what universities are for, or that they are mainly for the economy. Like any occupational group academics are far from homogenous; they differ along axes of type of institution, discipline, seniority, gender, race, social class, able-bodiedness, and nationality. To take just one example of the diverse positioning of academics, Goddard (2003) and Utley (2003) writing in the *Times Higher Education Supplement* compared the views of a handful of academics from an élite university in London (University College, London), and a former polytechnic, now a university, in the north of England (Teeside). They asked them what universities are for. From UCL, Mary Fulbrook, Professor of German, said that a university 'has to have space for debate and discussion and reading and thinking. If you are thinking about blue-skies research you cannot predict what will come up. It is also really crucial and an aspect of the human condition to think about who we are – space for that has to be preserved not only for those already doing it but also for young people to flower and explore and think'. Her colleague, David Colquhoun, Professor of Pharmacology, was of the view that: 'It's about truth and having people who are willing to study questions dispassionately and think abstractly about questions. The more we make everything dependent on numbers and things we can measure, the less room there is for independent thinkers'. At the University of Teeside, media studies lecturer Leo Enticknap commented 'The idea that academics are seekers after truth is too dogmatic. Universities ought to be seeking the ability to form valid judgements. This is enormously valuable to employers along with other generic skills you expect to pick up'. The tension between economically desirable pursuits and the expansion of the mind was never far from the surface in discussions about what universities are for, said Greg Reid, a lecturer in public health also at Teeside, while psychologist Ali Guy thought that: 'We have come to a workable compromise between elements of intellectual inquiry, which are valuable in their own right, and operating in a real world context, in which students are expected to gain transferable skills that will improve their employment prospects'.

Here we have common elements across academic opinion but also arguably some views inflecting more towards the issue of employability and the vocational aspects of higher education and others more towards the intrinsic goods of learning. This is not to judge one view as more or less relevant or better than another; rather it is to highlight that there are different perspectives or weightings on what is valuable about higher education. There is not one hegemonic mantra. Utley (2003) further elicited comment from a range of university 'stakeholders' and members of the public. While these comments cannot be held to be representative, nonetheless they do suggest the diversity of public opinion in England on what universities are for. For example: a sixth form (year 13) student from a London comprehensive school thought that 'University trains you for work and for life'; an employer from a direct marketing company was concerned with the proliferation of 'pseudo-academic subjects'; a doctor thought that the benefits of higher education 'are not measurable financially, [but] rather in an informed electorate able to debate issues and impart knowledge'; a taxi driver wondered how worthwhile a university education is when so many graduates seem to be out of work; and finally, a pensioner said that a university 'is not a sausage machine to turn out people whose only aim in life is to make money or boost the economy'. Thus we have here views ranging from the advantage of a university education as qualifications for employability, to the social and educational value of university learning.

Nonetheless, we might still argue that there are converging policy trends in higher education including the application of human capital theory, which prioritizes the economic returns from higher education. Simply put, human capital theory views education as an investment to improve productivity and the level and distribution of individual earnings. The origin of the idea of human capital, according to Angela Little (2003), goes back to Adam Smith's *Wealth of Nations* and the idea that investment in physical capital (machines) might have a parallel in investment in the productive capacity of human beings (human capital) through education. Little explains that the idea of investment in education for economic growth was revived by economists Theodore Schultz and Howard Becker in the early 1960s as a way to explain the puzzle of economic growth that could not be accounted for by increases in physical capital. Foreshadowing notions of a 'knowledge economy', attempts began from the 1960s to measure the economic costs and benefits of education as investments in human capital. Woodhall sums up:

> It implies that it is possible to measure the returns to education, and to apply cost benefit analysis to decisions about education expenditure in the same way as rates of return are used to analyse the profitability of investment in conventional physical capital.
>
> (2001: 6952, quoted in Little, 2003: 438)

Of course the assumption is that economic growth and development mean the same thing, and that both equal well-being. Yet, a recent Mori social survey in the UK exploring what makes people 'happiest' also confirms the burgeoning evidence from economists that doubling GDP in over 30 years in Britain has not made people any happier (Toynbee, 2004: 23, and see Gaspar, 2004). Nor does human capital theory explain why people make decisions to invest in education, or more education, or indeed to gainsay such investment (Little, 2003). Nonetheless the effect of human capital theory for higher education has been to ascribe the primary value of higher education to the extent that investment in individual students gives rise to increased economic productivity and higher incomes and augmented national wealth (Tight, 1996; Flores-Crespo, 2004).

Contemporary patterns in higher education include, in brief: the drive to demonstrate efficiency gains, value for money and closer links to the world of business; greater public accountability accompanied by regulatory mechanisms for compliance in teaching and research productivity; declining investment of public funds and the pressure to diversify institutional sources of income; competition amongst universities; the dominance of managerial forms of governance and performative cultures and entrepreneurial approaches; employability and labour market responsive vocationalized curricula; and the commodification of knowledge (see Stromquist, 2002; Naidoo, 2003; Peters, 2004). The 'good life' is then envisaged as the accumulation of material goods, a highly individualized notion of the citizen, and democracy as synonymous with capitalism, consumerism and the unrestrained pursuit of profit.

For an ethical discourse

Yet there is also space and indeed some urgency to challenge human capital discourse as a way of talking and thinking about higher education and to reassert an ethical and moral discourse. Burmese pro-democracy activist Aung San Suu Kyi (1995: 18, quoted in Nnaemeka, 2003: 37) reminds us that the 'true development of human beings involves much more than mere economic growth'. There is still the possibility for higher education and universities to make a difference to the viability and quality of the societies in which they are located and to human flourishing as an intrinsic good, as well as preparation for work. It is the former that is now rarely asserted in the face of growing pressures on higher education to be more responsive to economic development and the knowledge society (Peters, 2004). Nelly Stromquist (2002: 128) reminds us there are many challenges facing us in attaining the positive potential of universities. They are, she says 'unfortunately, numerous', but summed up in two key challenges: (i) 'to create and offer learning environments that foster students' development of intercultural adaptability and human solidarity'; and, (ii) 'a responsibility to engage the rest of society in a critical understanding of ongoing economic and political developments throughout the world' (2002: 130). At stake in the face of neo-liberal market reforms and the language in education of measurable performance indicators, learning objectives and predetermined outcomes, audit and regulation, is the need boldly and imaginatively to assert alternative frames of understanding and to defend public values in higher education. As Lyndsey Paterson's (2000) wide-ranging historical review of developments in higher education in Europe notes, higher education builds social capital for civil society. Indeed, Paterson argues that higher education is best placed of the education sectors to do this, given the greater maturity of its students.

I turn now to three persuasive examples which present counter-discourses about higher education, and which in turn enable us to generate different questions about its purposes. Firstly, Martha Nussbaum (1997, 2002) has produced a detailed account of liberal education in the USA, taking us onto diverse university campuses and into classrooms in different subject areas. She defends a Socratic view of education, which places the examined life at its centre, Aristotle's notion of reflective citizenship, and the Stoic view of an education that is liberal in that it frees us from habit and custom to function with sensitivity and awareness in the world. She argues that the cultivation of humanity is central to a liberal higher education, and establishes three core values and capacities of liberal higher education: critical self-examination, the ideal of the world citizen, and the development of the narrative imagination. The first is a capacity for critical examination of oneself and one's traditions – the 'examined life' – which requires a critical perspective on our beliefs, traditions and habits, reasoning logically and testing ideas for consistency, correctness and accuracy of judgement as a democratic citizen. Secondly, Nussbaum argues, we need to develop the ability to see ourselves not only as belonging to a local community, but also as bound to all other human beings 'by ties of recognition and concern in a global world' (1997: 10). Thirdly, is the cultivation of a 'narrative imagination', by which Nussbaum means the ability to think what it might be like to be in the place of a person different from oneself, to read such people's stories intelligently, and to understand the emotions and desires that someone so placed might have. Nussbaum is advocating a higher education which develops each person's capacity 'to be fully human' (2002: 290). Following Seneca, this means someone who is: 'self-aware, self-governing, and capable of recognizing and respecting the humanity of all our fellow human beings, no matter where they are born, no matter what social class they inhabit, no matter what their gender or ethnic origin' (2002: 290). The rise of narrowly vocational programmes in higher education risks, for example, students, parents and university managers viewing learning as the enrichment of life as a costly irrelevance. Yet, she declares, 'People who have never learned to use reason and imagination to enter a broader world of cultures, groups and ideas are impoverished personally and politically, however successful their vocational preparation' (1997: 297).

In a second example, Richard Taylor, Jean Barr and Tom Steele (2002) argue for a 'radical' higher education as a challenge to the way in which higher education is being incorporated into the world of corporate capital. They point to the pervasive context of inequality and capitalist hegemony in contemporary society and its influences on higher education policy and practices. Universities constitute part of the public sphere and while, they argue, no public sphere can be entirely independent of current market ideology and political economy, 'the inherently contradictory pressures of the system mean that alternative and oppositional forces can and do form discrete spaces of their own' (2002: 15). They argue for the open contestation of knowledges and values, and utilize the languages of political and social theory, philosophy, cultural studies and contemporary history, and perspectives from socialist, feminist and liberal theoretical perspectives to tell their story of higher education. They advocate a higher education that fosters the development of individuals capable of leading 'fulfilling and responsible lives and who have a reflexive grasp of what is in the best interests of themselves, their families, their communities and their society' (2002: 161).

My third example is taken from the widely known work of Ronald Barnett (1997, 2000, 2003) who emphasizes the centrality of 'critical being' and 'criticality' to a socially responsive higher education, by which he means an integration of critical thinking, critical action in the world and critical reflection. Barnett (1997: 7) argues that if higher education does not develop and practise critical being, society 'will then be diminished as a rational society and as a self-transforming society'. More recently, he (2003) has developed a compelling argument for enabling and building virtuous *idea*logies (of engaged universities, uniting teaching and research and reasonableness) and ideals of generosity, openness, self-critique, reasonableness, tolerance and imagination in modern universities as a counter to the pernicious ideologies (entrepeneurialism, competition, quality, managerialism) that have come to dominate. Barnett (2003: 176) writes that: 'Ideologies are quietened by new counter-energies being released on campus'; he hopefully suggests that 'creative efforts' may weaken 'pernicious ideologies'.

The capability approach applied in higher education, and specifically in the case of this book to higher education pedagogy, offers, I believe, a similar challenge to human capital discourse, and as I hope to show, ways to take our thinking and practice forward in a progressive direction.

Pedagogy

Before proceeding to flesh out the key ideas from the capability approach for higher education, a word about matters of pedagogy more generally. The patterns in higher education noted above, and the emphasis on education for human capital and economic policy, also impact on policy and practices of pedagogy in universities. Lingard (2005: 1) has written about 'thinned out pedagogies which result from the cold rapture of the market'. Market idolatry is captured in higher education's contemporary dominant emphasis on: 'knowledge is money' (Bernstein, 2000: 86); decontextualized transferable and key skills; measurable learning activities and outcomes; the splitting of teaching from research (see Barnett, 2003); processes of 'quality' assurance of teaching (see Morley, 2003); lecturer training to improve teaching; and, a discourse of teaching and learning rather than curriculum and pedagogy. Of course, how one is to measure and quantify the goods a higher *education* ought to produce, or how instrumental pedagogies are to support universities' claims as places 'of debate, of openness . . . in which ideas ferment and persons can flourish' (Barnett, 2003: 177) is then open to question.

But against such thinned-out versions of pedagogy, my purpose in this book is to claim pedagogy in higher education for ethical purposes. I take pedagogy to mean the method of teaching in the widest sense, that is, it extends beyond only the role of the lecturer or teacher. It involves not only who teaches, but also who is taught (and of course is interwoven with what is taught – the curriculum), and the contextual conditions under which such teaching and learning takes place. Moreover, pedagogic action involves a relationship of power in the transfer of knowledge (Bourdieu and Passeron, 1977). Davis (2004) helpfully traces an etymology of 'pedagogy' which combines notions of didactics (the teacher's technical role) with pedagogy (the moral and ethical). He explains:

> In some European languages other than English, pedagogy is paired up with didactics to describe the role of the teacher. Neither word has a direct English translation. Didactics is roughly synonymous with instructional techniques or methods, but is also used to refer to the teacher's command of the subject matter knowledge, ability to interpret student responses, and other personal competencies. In complement, pedagogy, is more a reference to the teachers' interpersonal competencies, and is thus used to refer to the moral and ethical – as opposed to the technical – aspects of the teacher's work with learners. It is this sense of responsibility to learners that prompted many critical education theorists to adopt the noun pedagogy . . .
>
> (2004: 143–144)

Teaching approaches or methods and student learning are therefore socially inflected by the identities of teacher and students, institutionally situated, and influenced by curricular aims and design. It is an interactive, relational space between lecturers and students, and students and students, where knowledge is mediated, where power circulates, and social and institutional structures penetrate. How to teach (and what to teach) is furthermore a practical expression of whether existing cultural, economic and political patterns in any society ought to be reproduced or transformed. Thus there is always the possibility of either normalizing and reproducing social and cultural inequalities and oppressive power relations, or for 'moments of equity' (Berge and Ve, 2000) in which transformation is achieved. This, I argue, is a social justice issue in higher education. Michael Apple (2001) usefully points to the particular kinds of morality which underpin competing versions of education. On the one hand, he argues, a 'thick morality' is grounded in notions of the common good as the ethical basis for policy and practice, while a 'thin morality' is grounded in competitive individualism and hierarchical divisions. Put another way would be to ask whether the purpose of higher education pedagogy holds ethical values to be central, as much as the development of knowledge and skills, that is, *both* ethics *and* gaining knowledge. In short, what does it mean for a person to become educated, and what is a worthwhile process of higher education? If we take higher education to be a social good, which contributes to the democratization of the polity, such aims and purposes will influence pedagogic decisions and practices and knowledge and learning outcomes, in some way. Therefore if we are committed to higher education as a public good and to public values we need to pay attention to the framing of our educational purposes and their pedagogic realisation.

To further link back into my earlier argument for the importance of higher education and a criterion of justice, I also want to say a brief word about the notion of Ernest Boyer's (1990) idea of the 'scholarship of teaching', often invoked to bolster arguments around the importance of teaching at universities. This is a worthwhile deployment of his ideas, but what is seldom mentioned by those who take up this particular claim, at least in the UK, is also Boyer's earlier call for greater attention to the moral and civic purposes of higher education (albeit in his case in the USA). In his report on the undergraduate experience, Boyer (1987) wrote:

> Throughout our study we were impressed that what today's college is teaching most successfully is competence . . . But technical skill of whatever kind, leaves open essential questions: Education for what purpose? Competence to what end? At a time in life when values should be shaped and personal priorities sharply probed, what a tragedy it would be if the most deeply felt issues, the most haunting questions, the most creative moments were pushed to the fringes of our institutional life. What a monumental mistake it would be if students, during the undergraduate years, remained trapped in the organisational grooves and narrow routines to which the academic world sometimes seems excessively devoted.
>
> (1987: 283, quoted in Colby *et al.*, 2003: 6)

Pedagogies, then, for competence plus wise judgement.

I need further to say what this book is not about. It is not my intention: to provide an exhaustive overview of the higher education literature on 'approaches to learning' (for example, Entwistle and Ramsden, 1983; Marton and Booth, 1997; Biggs, 2003; Brockbank and McGill, 1998; Prosser and Trigwell, 1998, and see Haggis 2003 for a critique of this tradition)[1]; 'critical pedagogy' (for example, Freire 1972, 1978 and 1985; McLaren, 1989 and 1995; Giroux, 1992; Lankshear and McLaren, 1993; hooks, 1994; Leistyna *et al.* 1996; Kincheloe, 2004, and see Ellsworth 1989 for a critique); feminist pedagogy (for example, Belenky *et al.*, 1986; Weiler, 1988; Lather, 1991; Luke and Gore, 1992; Gore, 1993; Lewis, 1993; Ropers-Huilman, 1998; Ryan, 2001), or to synthesize these different approaches to teaching and learning as Mann (2001), Ashwin and McLean (2004), Pollard (2003) and work in academic literacies (for example, Lea and Street, 1998; Scott, 2004) attempt in interesting ways. Nor will I review philosophical accounts, for example Barnett (1997, 2003) and Blake, Smith and Standish (1998), or work which stands at the nexus of philosophies of university teaching and practice, of which Stephen Rowland's work is a fine example (Rowland, 2000). Nor do I plan to offer an account of disciplinary-based pedagogy (but see Phipps and Gonzalez, 2004 for an excellent example), or suggest practical ideas on how to teach in order to improve learning.

Having said that, ideas from critical pedagogy have influenced my thinking over the years in so far as they challenge us to critique undemocratic social practices and institutional structures, with a view to transforming them through action and reflection (*praxis*). Undemocratic practices and power relations produce inequalities and distort identity formation in acknowledging some identities and not others, and admitting some meanings and not others (Leistyna *et al.*, 1996). Critical pedagogy foregrounds relations of power and education as a form of cultural politics, in which typical questions for educational practice might include the following: How do students come to know the subject? Do they participate actively and democratically as individuals and collectively with their peers? Are student experiences used as points of critical access and connections to academic knowledge? Are students enabled to understand and to challenge knowledge? Are some voices excluded from knowledge and learning? Do students come to understand the world as constructed and open to change by human agents? Do students develop their critical awareness of themselves, of knowledge and of the relationships between self, knowledge and the wider world? (Leistyna and Woodrum, 1999). These are important questions and I return to them in later chapters when I consider narratives of student learning.

At this point, I will briefly consider two accounts of pedagogy as exemplars of studies which search theoretically and practically for an ethical language for higher education pedagogy, connecting broader social trends with student learning opportunities and outcomes, and suggesting hopeful possibilities for the future. I explore them thus as models for discussing higher education pedagogy which are philosophical, ethical and practical at some level. In their account of higher education pedagogy as 'teaching for supercomplexity', Barnett and Hallam (1999) take up what they regard as a silence around pedagogical issues in the 1997 government-commissioned *Dearing Report* on higher education in the UK. They develop an approach which tries to integrate teaching approaches and conceptions and learning with the aims of higher education in a context of globalization and shifts to a 'learning society'. From this they generate a normative theory of the kinds of pedagogical processes appropriate to the twenty-first century, one which they characterize as a world of 'supercomplexity', and it is here that they locate their philosophical conceptualisations. In a supercomplex world we face dilemmas of understanding the world, of action in the world, and of self-understanding in that world. There are resonances here with Barnett's (1997) earlier notion of critical being and criticality but supercomplexity seeks to take this idea further. It considers the way lecturers and students are faced with multiple and contesting frameworks of interpretation through which to make sense of one's world and to act purposively within it. Supercomplexity describes the incommensurability and irreconcilability of competing values and positions in the contemporary western world. The effects for pedagogy are as follows:

> If we are faced with an inchoate, unpredictable and continually challenging world, then graduates will have to have powers of self-reliance in

order to cope with and to act purposively in that world. Responsibility is placed on the self for surviving in an uncertain world. In turn, if this call is to be heeded, pedagogies in higher education will presumably need to be those that foster such human qualities.

(Barnett and Hallam, 1999: 138)

What they mean is that students 'have in some way to fashion some kind of stability where no stability is available' in the domains of knowledge, action and self (1999: 148). Thus they argue that a pedagogy for supercomplexity needs to be based on a view of learning construed 'as the acquisition of those human capabilities appropriate for adaptation to conditions of radical and enduring uncertainty, unpredictability, challengeability and contestability' (1999: 142). They suggest that the domains of knowledge and action are recognized as pedagogical domains in higher education but much less recognized is that of the self (or we might also say, education's role in identity formation). But without attention to self/identity they suggest agency, as the capacity to effect purposive change in one's environment will be diminished because 'the self will be liable not to be a subject of its destiny but its object' (1999: 149). The task and responsibility for higher education is then:

> to prepare students fully for a world of uncertainty, challenge and turbulence. Appropriate pedagogies for such a world are not to be caught by the talk of the production of competences and skills, however 'generic' or 'transferable'. Instead they will be pedagogies that enable graduates purposively to effect change in that world, and to have the enduring will to do so, even though those graduates realise – through their higher education – that there can in such a world be no final warrant for their actions and claims, and their own sense of self.
>
> (1999: 151–2)

The second account I now consider is from Sarah Mann's (2001) work on the student experience, using the theoretical language of alienation and engagement to reframe 'approaches to learning' and to explore some of the different ways we might understand an alienated experience of learning and how it might arise. She aligns herself with Barnett's (1997) notion of critical being as the prime purpose for higher education, and describes this for her own purposes as involving 'personal engagement, inclusion and lifelong learning' (2001: 7–8). With this broad aim in mind, her own focus is on student experiences of learning as either alienated or engaged. She develops seven different theoretical perspectives on alienation. The first of these she names as the postmodern condition in which alienation 'is viewed as inevitable' (2001: 8) under contemporary social and cultural conditions. Performativity, utility, efficiency, education as consumption all replace ideals of emancipation or truth and conditions of complexity, estranging students from personal purposefulness and 'from an intrinsic pursuit of knowledge, understanding or justice through education' (2001: 9). The second frame arises from the student's being positioned in discursive practices in particular ways, thereby constraining (controlling, determining) how they may act and be in higher education, with inevitable alienation effects. The third frame considers students as strangers or migrants in the foreign world of higher education, and this would be most apparent among non-traditional entrants such as working class students or mature women learners. Such students face the choice of either assimilation or rejection of the colonising process, 'whether to join in or not and at what cost' (2001: 11). They are estranged from the academy and themselves and must repress 'the very selves they may need for engaging in learning' (2001: 12).

The fourth frame explores the experience of alienation from the perspective of creativity as opposed to compliance where creativity is understood to involve active and meaningful ways of being. But learning and power relationships in higher education, argues Mann, do not foster creativity and an autonomous, authentic self so that the student develops a false self as a means of survival. The student is estranged from her 'creative and autonomous self as a learner, replaced by a compliant self unable to access the vitality of their creative self, and acquiescing to the demands and prescriptions of their course requirements' (2001: 13). The fifth frame draws on Marx's concept of alienation to explain how students produce work (labour) in exchange for a grade. The student belongs to the work (essay), rather than the work belonging to the student. Following Marx the student is alienated in four ways: from the product of her labour, from the process of producing the work, from her own voice and self as a human being and from other human beings under institutional conditions of the distribution of power and ownership in higher education. The sixth frame addresses assessment from a Foucauldian frame. Here Mann considers the way power is expressed through the examination, which makes the student publicly visible and objectifies him or her in an unequal relationship of power with the examiner, and the confession in which the student is subjectified by the more powerful Other who listens and judges. Both technologies position students in a hierarchy of success relative to other students and expertise relative to the teacher/examiner. They are produced as this kind of student (high achieving, clever, pleasant), or that kind of student (mediocre, inarticulate, surly). Alienation is then one means of survival. In her final frame she further explores alienation as a means of survival, and suggests that for (some) students 'it is much safer not to engage' (2001: 15), to distance oneself from thinking and learning and the constant normalising judgement of the self that this involves.

Mann considers the gap experienced between the identity of being a student or teacher and who we want to be, and the tensions this dissonance generates. One means of survival for students she suggests is to take surface approaches to learning, rather than to risk the self through the uncertainty of active, creative and engaged participation in learning. What Mann's approach does is to locate student learning and university teaching contextually within broader shifts in higher education and society. She theoretically reframes ideas of deep, surface and strategic learning to generate an alternative way of understanding student learning which raises implications for changing pedagogical practices in the direction of the just and the ethical. Using an elaborated framing of alienation and conceptualizations of power, repression, play, creative engagement, and the student self she elucidates 'the complex relations of power that exist within the educational and teaching/learning process' (2001: 17). Her theoretical frames open out five responses for educational change, described as: 'solidarity' (dissolving the estrangement between us and them), 'hospitality' (welcoming newcomers to the academy), 'safety' (safe spaces for learning), 'redistribution of power', and 'criticality'. She regards this last response 'as a crucial way out of the experience of alienation' through becoming aware of the conditions of higher education and how we respond to them, and to act on this awareness: 'Such awareness and the capacity to act on that awareness, must arise out of criticality – the capacity and opportunity to question, examine, uncover, reframe, make visible and interpret' (2001: 17–18). She cites Barnett's (1997: 171–2) argument for 'critical energy' – the will on the part of the students to invest themselves in their engagement with thinking, self and action – and argues that this is what we need to inspire in higher education 'through a teaching and learning relationship based on an ethical position' (2001: 18) in which the 'I' of the teacher is fundamentally responsible for the 'other' of the student. Mann argues that her five responses to alienation would form the basis of such an ethical shift in the teaching/learning relationship and a move to 'the criterion of justice as a value in education' (2001: 18).

What both these studies do, I suggest, is to demonstrate how the way we conceptually and discursively frame our accounts of pedagogy and learning produces one narrative rather than another. In Barnett and Hallam's case the central idea of supercomplexity produces one approach to thinking about pedagogy; in the case of Mann the key idea of alienation produces another pedagogical story. But in both cases, the framing opens out possibilities for making futures, for agency and for engaged learning in higher education pedagogy. Using the capability approach as a central framing idea, I wish to attempt a similar conceptual storying of higher education pedagogy, one which broadly intersects with both these approaches in that it will address engaged learning, agency, and change, and like Mann, a deep ethical concern with the development of each and every student as an end in themselves. But more than this there will be more explicit attention to a language and practice of agency and social choice, to equality and justice in higher education pedagogy, and to the relationship between higher education and society. I foreground the idea of equality deliberately as 'the *condition* of being equal in quantity, value, intensity, privileges' (Shorter Oxford English Dictionary, 1973: 673), that is, equality is understood as a difficult practical matter of how broader inequalities penetrate and shape the educational arena. It includes, but is more than, equity (fairness, even-handedness) which opens up educational opportunities for all. We should be accountable in higher education for equality, including acting when we fall short. It is to ask, following Sen (1992), 'equality of what?'. The capability approach raises crucial questions for what we mean by '[educational] development' and how we might compare the quality of the higher education experiences between students by considering their own valued achievements, rather than achievement as measured by policy-makers or institutions, or input-output measures (Unterhalter, 2003a). The question is less how do we teach and how do our students learn, but how might higher education contribute through such practices of teaching and learning to human flourishing. The pedagogical process is taken to be an ethical project of critical discourse, creative thinking, engaged learning and commitments to a democratic ethos and a rich and vibrant public life in the twenty-first century. At issue in general is how the capability approach 'provides a new perspective for addressing distributional issues and concerns with education equality' (Unterhalter, 2003a: 668). In taking this up in relation to pedagogy, I also seek to rework the boundaries between educational action and conceptual critique.

Mine is a project, then, which asks, 'Where is higher education's contribution to an equitable, just and humane democracy?' It stands against the alienation so eloquently described by Mann (2001), and as a counter to neo-liberal policies and human capital policies in higher education. It takes some encouragement from examples within higher education, such as the recent statement by Michael Worton, Vice-Provost of University College, London that his university has a duty to reach out and to solve the world's problems, 'to make a difference', and 'to make sure that all its students are learning what it means to be a global citizen' (quoted in Hodges, 2005: 6). The key issue at stake in the capabilities approach is to ask what it is that human beings require in order to live a richly human life. In her thought-provoking essay on Henry James' novel, *The Princess Casamassima*, Nussbaum (1990) takes up the argument of Hyacinth Robinson, the novel's working class hero, that any real solution to the problems of poverty and inequality in the world (from which higher education ought not to turn away) 'must take place in the context of an ongoing sense of life's richness and value and full humanity' (Nussbaum, 1990: 211). If higher education ought to enable human flourishing, we must then go on to ask how in and through higher education we support rather than diminish such flourishing.

This book further assumes that this matter of human flourishing and a life of human dignity is a matter for public policy, given the demonstrated effects on society of the wider benefits of learning. For example, in the UK, Tom Schuller and his colleagues (Schuller *et al.*, 2002) point to the sustaining effect of education on personal lives and the social fabric. Education, they argue 'transforms people's lives' (2002: vii) and enables them to cope with everyday life and social change, to contribute to the well-being of others and to maintain community and collective life. They argue further that learning 'is of fundamental importance in sustaining and improving communication at every level and in every form' (vii), and that educational institutions (including universities) are places where people can participate in a culture of learning. Moreover, their studies show the wider benefits of learning for people's health and mental well-being and for family learning. While this research considers all stages of learning across a life course, we could none-theless still argue that such wider benefits of learning for individuals and society are also a matter for public policy in higher education. This is not quite the same as arguing that higher education is unequivocally a public good, or that it necessarily serves all members of society equally. As Ruth Jonathan (2001) shows in a closely argued essay, the case of higher education as a public good is not so straightforward. She explains that higher education is not a wholly public good in the same way, say, that a stable monetary system is, but nor is it a wholly private enterprise in that higher education is not produced and distributed solely by individuals without co-operation with others. She usefully sums up the case by arguing that higher education is a *social* good: it is not universally accessible; it conveys public and private benefits; its private benefits give rise to a broad range of other goods which are public, private and social. For example, not everyone will be able to study medicine (or indeed wish to) and qualify to work as a general practitioner. This qualification certainly confers financial and status benefits on the indi-vidual,[2] but also public and social benefits in working for the public sector. However, argues Jonathan, we need to hold on to the insight from this somewhat unhelpful public versus private good debate that, 'any social prac-tice which is basic both to the future development of society and to the individual life-chances of its citizens is the proper business of the democratic state' (2001: 31).

We can then move on, she says to consider which matters are important and relevant if higher education is to advance the public good. My particular concern is then with the specificity of pedagogies. For example, to return to the student studying medicine at university, the question might be some-thing like, how do we contribute through our pedagogical and curriculum work in higher education to the formation of women and men who can acquire the relevant knowledge, think theoretically, analyse with rigour and also act ethically, with a social conscience and care for public life? Here I would wish to emphasize that I do not have in mind forcing student doctors to become this sort of professional, instead of that. Rather I have in mind Hannah Arendt's (1977) notion that our work in higher education ought to make it at least possible for students to act on the future differently and to renew the common world. Arendt writes that, 'The problem is simply to educate in such a way that a setting-right [of the world] remains actually possible, even though of course, it can never be assured' (1977: 192). The point is that higher education, as with the schooling that precedes it, involves a remaking of self, a process of identity formation, as new knowledge and understandings develop and previous knowledge of self and of the world is reframed in a process of learning. But we cannot guarantee that this refram-ing will occur, or insist that it occurs in the way we might wish. We can, however, provide the pedagogical conditions – 'educate in such a way' – that educational development that supports human flourishing is enabled.

Introducing the capability approach

It is from this point that this book now proceeds. It does so by placing a particular theoretical framework, Amartya Sen's (1992, 1999, 2002) capability approach, at the centre of its discussion and analysis and attempts to show what this framework can add to existing approaches to higher education development and change, particularly pedagogy and student learning. I argue in this book for a capability-based approach as pointing to a criterion of justice in higher education, or more ambitiously, to develop a capability-based theory of social justice in higher education. There are as yet very few projects in education specifically which take up the capability approach. Clearly in the broader capability literature education is often touched on but not explored in detail. In the area of gender justice Unterhalter (2001, 2003a, 2003b, 2004a, 2004b), Unterhalter and Brighouse (2003), Vaughan (2004), Walker (2002a, 2003, 2004a, 2004b) and George (2004) have taken up the capability approach. Teacher development is being considered by Page (2004) and Raynor (2004), special education by Terzi (2003, 2004), school leadership by Bates (2004), adult literacy by Alkire (2002), and education in general by Saito (2003), Biggeri *et al.* (2004), and Flores Crespo (2004). In the specific field of higher education there is as yet a very small body of work (Flores-Crespo, 2001; Deprez and Butler, 2001; Watts and Bridges 2003; Bozalek, 2004), none of which specifically addresses pedagogy but which does raise some of the key issues which I explore. These will be taken up in the chapters which follow.

The starting point of the capability approach is Sen's argument (1992: 295) that, 'if we focus on the expansion of human freedom instead of focusing on economic progress as an end of education endeavours, then economic growth can be integrated into a foundational understanding of the process of development as the expansion of human capability to lead more worthwhile and more free lives'. Human capability is then at the heart of development. But, Des Gaspar and Irene Van Staveren (2003) do point out that the more common use of capability is as a skill or an aptitude, and they argue for the importance of S-capability (skills) as well as O-capability (opportunity). In other words capabilities are a combination of skills and opportunities. These ideas will be elaborated in the chapters which follow. They are raised at this early point simply to make clear and to emphasise what I mean in this book when I talk about capability and capabilities. At the outset it is important therefore to stress that Sen's notion of human capability is somewhat different from that of the Higher Education Capability Forum (HEC), based in the UK (see Stephenson and Weil, 1992). Capability is of course a fairly everyday term and this generates the possibility for confusion in higher education where the notion of capability has been claimed by HEC as skills, competence, experiential and work-based learning and a thin, largely uncritical notion of the 'autonomous learner' as a self-managing consumer. HEC seeks to address what it takes as a worrying split between the idea of education and that of training in universities so that young people acquire knowledge and the skills of scholarship, HEC argues in its Capability Manifesto (1988: 1), but 'are not equipped to use knowledge in ways which are relevant to the world outside the education system'.

This injunction to bring higher education into a closer relationship with the outside world and the world of work is of course not necessarily problematic. What is at issue is the purposes for such a relationship and the effects of these differing purposes for teaching and learning. Barr (2002) argues against the splitting of theory and practice where debating the world's problems is divorced from participating in activities that might solve those same problems. She argues thus for the university's social engagement with its public and an acknowledgement of the validity of experiences and knowledges located outside the academy. Practical projects are then a source of insight and knowledge. Yet too many academics, Barr (2002: 330) asserts, decry the practices and problems of everyday life. A liberally educated person may care deeply about knowledge, ideas and argument 'but have no desire to solve real problems in the real world'. Barr's ethical argument for an engaged university and an orientation to social justice is, however, rather different from a narrower technicist focus on a rather compliant relationship between higher education and the world of work which is oriented to addressing economic needs and the skills shortage in the global marketplace. Barr's perspective would be compatible with the capability approach; while the latter view would be an unacceptably narrow interpretation of human capability. Following Arendt's (1977: 196) emphasis on the importance of enabling our students the opportunity to undertake something new, 'something foreseen by no-one', Raymond Gaita (2000: 43) explains that teachers who insist on making what they teach 'relevant' to their students' future needs as these are 'divined' by government, deny this chance of 'newness' to their students.

For Sen (1992, 1999, 2002), then, human capability has a distinct meaning. His ideas are explored in detail in the next chapter, suffice to note here some of his key points. The term capability means 'not skills but attainable options' and 'a language of freedom' (Gaspar and Van Staveren, 2003: 144, 145). The central idea in the approach which will be elaborated in the chapters that follow is that development should focus on what people are actually able to be and do, personally and in comparison to others. In higher education we might then ask what diverse graduates able to be and do. But more than this the capability approach focuses on people's own reflective, informed choice of ways of living that they deem important and valuable, and the self-determination of ends and values in life. This contrasts to human capital approaches which measure the value of higher education in terms of its national economic returns and impact on Gross Domestic Product. Agency is a central idea for Sen, and is closely connected to human wellbeing. Thus the idea of choice is central but takes its meaning from the justice and equality principles of the capability approach, not from neoliberal thinking. The individual is not viewed as a freely choosing subject;

constraints on choice are acknowledged if arguably under-theorized socio-
logically (see Unterhalter, 2001, 2003a, 2003b). Certainly Sen argues that
each individual counts but he also argues for the relationship and intercon-
nections of the individual, the institutional and the social in enabling
opportunities and valued choices. He foregrounds diversity as integral to
human life, not an add-on and points to the limits of assessing equality
simply by considering what resources people or nations have. Their capability to convert these resources into capability is at issue. This emphasis on
development for more than economic growth further emphasizes the
intrinsic value and role of (higher) education. The approach acknowledges
the difficulties with people's subjective wants and that these might be
adapted in ways which do not necessarily serve the best interests of the
chooser, for example women might adapt their ambitions in a culture where
maleness has more prestige and cultural power. The approach is multi-
dimensional requiring us to take into account a range of capabilities, how
they intersect and how one capability is important for the development of
another. Finally, Sen does not specify a list of capabilities and this then raises
the theoretical and practical problem of whether the capability approach
needs a well-defined list of capabilities.

As noted earlier, there is very little that has been written on the capability
approach and education, even less on the capability approach and higher
education. Additionally education is under-theorized in the capability
approach. I take these issues up in Part 2, where the core ideas from the
capability approach for education are presented. I then consider the issue of
what we are distributing in higher education, in other words, what is it we are
evaluating when we consider equality and development in higher education?
I proceed to Part 3 and apply the capability approach to suggest its possibilities. I do this by exploring a process to generate a higher education list
of human capabilities and showing how we might use such a list to evaluate
in/equality in teaching and learning. I first apply Nussbaum's (2000a) view
of human capabilities to widening participation students and their learning.
Then I explore illustrative instances of pedagogy and student learning.
These 'capability narratives' draw on examples which are illustrative rather
than comprehensive, that is they do not seek to cover the full range of
disciplines in higher education but rather to explore possibilities. In the final
chapter I draw together the ideas, framing them as pedagogies for capability
and equality, in which a criterion of justice is central, and draw out what I
take to be the implications and possibilities for educational change and the
work of making futures.

The book leaves my argument open to challenge and to revision in the
light of further evidence and cases, but also opens up the capability
approach for debate and dialogue about what it has to offer theory and
practice in contemporary higher education. It is important to note that Sen,
himself has always stressed the incompleteness of his ideas (see Chapter 2
and Chapter 3), hence it is an approach, rather a theory of justice. It is
open to being taken up in diverse contexts and to being complemented by

additional theories, while still being 'a rich resource for thinking about education' (Unterhalter 2003a: 668). Above all, the book attempts to generate a hopeful discourse about higher education pedagogics. It seeks to remind practitioner and policy communities that higher education is not only an enabler of capabilities, but also constitutive of freedom and from this perspective, intrinsically valuable as an end in itself.

To close, I should also say at this point that this book assumes throughout that undergraduate education is core to the work and existence of universities (Rhodes, 1993), of diverse kinds across the global stage. Writing specifically of research universities, Rhodes (1993: 181)) further reminds us that it is through undergraduate education that universities encounter their publics most directly, and that it is on the health of teaching and learning that the research university 'will stand or fall'.

Notes

1 Because this research is so influential in the field of teaching and learning at least in the UK – it has successfully disseminated the now widespread notion of surface, deep and strategic learning, for example – it merits a few words. As Barnett and Hallam (1999) suggest, this body of cumulative research has demonstrated persuasively that the quality and character of the way that students are taught and the learning environment they experience impacts on the quality of their learning. University teachers, it then follows, must take on their professional responsibility as educators. In short, this literature has much to offer in improving learning and teaching in universities. But Barnett and Hallam qualify their approval by suggesting that this research is limited in three ways: (i) it assumes accepted and stable bodies of knowledge about which students come to a 'deep' understanding; (ii) it emphasizes the cognitive to the exclusion of the social in learning; and (iii) learning is understood to be somehow separate from students' own sense of self and learner identity is then overlooked. Also see Tamsin Haggis's (2003) interesting critique, and the subsequent response from Delia Marshall and Jennifer Case (2005).
2 Graduates in the UK for example still command significantly higher salaries than those without degrees, even given the recent expansion of higher education to a 47% entry rate. A recent OECD review for 2004 cited by Ward (2004: 11) found that British graduates earn 59% more than non-graduates, one of the highest degree premiums in the OECD. The review found that in countries with even higher rates of participation in higher education, such as Australia and Sweden, graduate salaries are holding steady or increasing.

Part 2

The Capability Approach and
Higher Education

2

Core Ideas from the Capability Approach

It will be seen how in place of the wealth and poverty of political economy come the rich human being and rich human need. The rich human being is simultaneously the human being in need of a totality of human life-activities – the person in whom his own realisation exists as an inner necessity, as need.

(Karl Marx, *Economic and Philosophical Manuscripts of 1844*)

This chapter and the one which follows do not set out to review theories of justice and to compare and contrast these with the capability approach, nor do they seek to review the by now burgeoning multi-disciplinary literature on the capability approach as a human development paradigm.[1] This is not a book on the capability approach but one on higher education pedagogies which seeks to adopt key ideas from the capability approach as a means to think about a criterion of justice in relation to 'teaching and learning' in higher education. Therefore what this chapter sets out to do is to explain the core ideas in the capability approach before showing in the following chapters how these ideas might be taken up in higher education as a location for the pedagogical mediation of knowledge.

Capability

Sen (1992, 1999, 2002) has produced the core concepts of capabilities and functioning as goals for the development of our full human dignity. By capability he means what people are actually free to be and do, rather than how much income they have. Sen (1992: 81) explains that: 'In the capability-based assessment of justice, individual claims are not to be assessed in terms of the resources or primary goods the persons respectively hold, but by the freedoms they actually enjoy to choose the lives that they have 'reason to value'. People should be able to make choices that matter to them for a valuable life. Capabilities might then also be explained as 'actions one values doing or approaches to living one's values' (Unterhalter, 2003a: 666).

A capability is a potential functioning – what one actually manages to achieve or do – and the list of functionings is endless. A functioning is 'the various things a person may value doing or being' (Sen, 1999: 75), it is the practical realization of one's chosen way of life. It might include quite basic functionings such as being well-nourished, having shelter and access to clean water and being physically safe, or more complex functioning like being well-educated, having paid professional work, being respected, taking part in discussions with your peers, being scientifically literate, and so on. The difference between a capability and functioning is like one between an opportunity to achieve and the actual achievement, between potential and outcome. For example, the capability for mobility and actually moving around, the capability to be literate compared to actually reading, or the capability to be well-educated and acting and being a well-educated person. All a person's capabilities together comprise her capability set, 'her real or substantive freedom to be and do what she wants' (Robeyns, 2003a: 544). For Sen, it is not so much the achieved functionings that matter, as the real opportunities (freedoms) that one has to achieve those functionings. Thus, the notion of capability, 'is essentially one of freedom – the range of options a person has in deciding what kind of life to lead' (Dreze and Sen, 1995: 11). Capability 'represents a person's freedom to achieve well being' (Sen, 1992: 48), so that 'acting freely and being able to choose are . . . directly conducive to well-being' (1992: 51). Sen (1992) further stresses the importance of choosing a life one has *reason* to value, that is a life reflectively chosen. At the same time, Sen cautions that increased choices do not necessarily lead to an increase in freedom if the options added are not ones we value. For example, the working class student who achieves good university entrance grades but who would rather become a plumber, valuing the activity, lifestyle and income it offers, has the freedom to choose university, but little reason to value access to higher education. While policy makers might see this as a perverse or awkward preference choice (as they attempt to meet widening participation targets), it is entirely intelligible to the young person for whom pressures to choose higher education may be unwelcome.

Sen (1992: 4–5) argues, then, that, 'A person's capability to achieve functionings that he or she has reason to value provides a general approach to the evaluation of social arrangements, and this yields a particular way of viewing the assessment of equality and inequality'. The distinction between capability and functioning is important. To return to the student who decides to become a plumber, even though she has the required grades for university entrance: she has the capability to choose. But another working class student who does not have the required grades and chooses plumbing, even though he would rather study engineering at university, does not have the same capability. On the surface the two students appear to have made a similar decision not to go to university. If one were evaluating only functionings (becoming a plumber) we would view the situation as the same. However, if we look at capabilities, we evaluate choices which for one of the students would have been different in other circumstances. As Unterhalter (2003a) points out, the first student has freedom and rationality; the second student has rationality in choosing plumbing but not accompanied by conditions of freedom. One could develop further examples around the specificity of pedagogy, with the crucial point being that our evaluation of equality must take account of freedom in opportunities as much as observed choices. The capability approach therefore offers a method to evaluate social (and hence for my purposes also educational) advantage. In this approach individual capabilities to undertake valued and valuable activities constitute an indispensable and central part of the relevant informational base of such an evaluation of advantage and disadvantage.

Functioning

There are cases, and education at all levels is arguably one such case, where it makes sense, however, also to consider people's functionings (what we manage to achieve) and not just their capabilities. For example, what if we are focusing on the capability of confidence in learning? We might plausibly assume that no one freely chooses to be an unconfident learner in higher education. If a student is then functioning as an unconfident learner, then this is a signal that their capability has not developed as they and we might wish. We might argue that during the course of their degree studies, universities and university teachers need to know if and how capability is being developed, by whom, and under what conditions. For example, University College, London is committing itself to student learning for global citizenship. We might describe this as a capability. But how will UCL know if they are succeeding in this aim if they do not consider how and whether their students are actually beginning to function in this way, that is, to show in some way while they are at university that they are developing this capability to be a global citizen? If after graduation they choose not to be global citizens, that is then another matter, if this is a reasoned choice. To take another example, the mediation and dissemination of knowledge is central to the work of a university. We would probably all say that we want students to have the capability for knowledge, usually of a specific subject area or professional field. But how will we know if we are succeeding without some evidence or information for their functioning as knowledgeable persons in the field of history, or physics, or mathematics? How do we adjust our own teaching if we have no understanding or information on what students are learning or becoming?

This is an important point for education and higher education in that it raises the tricky issue of whether we pay attention both to capability development and to functioning in education. At issue is how do we know that our students have valuable capabilities unless they are given opportunities to function and use these capabilities in educational situations. In terms of the informational base for making justice judgements, Sen (1992) argues that functionings give us information about the things a person does, while capabilities give us information about the things a person is substantively free to do (choose). But because capabilities are counter-factual – we cannot see a potential – we must then resort to functioning as a proxy for our assumptions about what capabilities are being fostered or diminished. The 'space' of capabilities is an evaluative space where what can be evaluated can be either realized functionings (what a person is actually able to do) or the capability set of alternatives she has (her real opportunities). As Gaspar and Van Staveren (2003: 148) point out, 'we must often measure capability via the proxy of functioning . . . for we need to measure functionings too if we are to evaluate human development adequately'. We are interested not only in whether a student has the potential and freedom to be confident about their learning, but also in how confident the student actually is. In professional education, we are interested not only in a student's potential to be a good teacher, but also in how good a teacher they actually are in practice settings. Thus the relationship between capability and functioning, certainly in education, is complicated, and this is therefore further explored in chapter 3.

One further element of Sen's capability approach should be borne in mind. It is concerned with the capabilities of each and very individual. But Sen's conceptualization is not to be confused with the neoliberal advocates of individualism and individual choice who dominate current higher education policy making. The crucial difference is that the capability approach is ethically individualistic; every individual matters and is of worth. Neoliberalism by contrast is ontologically individualist (Robeyns, 2003b). At issue is that Sen's work is informed by this ethical individualism – every diverse person counts – whereas the neo-liberal view grounded in ontological individualism is driven by selfish self-interest. As Robeyns (2003b: 44) explains, 'ethical individualism is not incompatible with an ontology that recognises the connections between people, their social relations, and their social embeddedness'. It is important to note, however, that a narrow interpretation of the capability approach might be combined with neo-liberal ideas to arrive at a different understanding. It is therefore important to consider additional theories, for example sociological theories which analyse the social structural constraints on choice, with the capability approach (Robeyns, 2003b).

The capability approach and educational analysis

Sen (1992, 1999, 2002), then, insists on the importance of *capabilities to function* in making normative evaluations about equality and well-being, rather than economic wealth and income as an indicator of a country's quality of life, or human capital theory which judges education only by its success in preparing participants for employment. Somewhat like 'Girl No 20' (in Charles Dickens' *Hard Times*), who was puzzled as to how overall national wealth could be equated to something called 'prosperity' without knowing who had got the money, and whether any of it was hers, for Sen, economic growth as an indicator of well-being does not help us to understand the barriers in our societies against equality for all. It does not tell us how well each person is doing, or what share of the resources they actually have access to.

The capability approach has not been developed as an educational theory but as an approach to human development and quality of life, particularly poverty reduction. Nonetheless, Sen (1992: 44) identifies education as one of 'a relatively small number of centrally important beings and doings that are crucial to well being'. He argues that education is an enabling factor in the expansion of freedom for five overlapping reasons. Like human capital approaches, Sen recognizes that education has an *instrumental* role for each person in helping him or her to do or achieve many things such as getting a job and being able to take up economic opportunities. Education is then for something else, for some other good. But in contrast to human capital approaches to education in which the benefit of education is directly judged for its effect on employability, Dreze and Sen (1995: 184) argue that the 'bettering of a human life does not have to be justified by showing that a person with a better life is also a better producer'. Education is of *intrinsic* importance in that being educated is a valuable achievement in itself, for its own sake. Education is in itself a basic capability; it is the foundation which affects the development and expansion of other capabilities. Having the opportunity for education and the development of an education capability expands human freedoms, that is, being able to choose to be and do what we value. Not having education harms human development and having a full life. It fulfils an *instrumental social role* in that critical literacy fosters public debate and dialogue about social and political arrangements. It has an *instrumental process role* by expanding the people one comes into contact with, broadening our horizons. Finally, it has an *empowering and distributive role* in facilitating the ability of the disadvantaged, marginalized and excluded to organize politically. It has redistributive effects between social groups, households and within families where better education is shown to reduce gender inequality. Overall, education contributes to interpersonal effects where people are able to use the benefits of education to help others and hence contribute to the social good and democratic freedoms. In short, for Sen, 'education' is an unqualified good for human capability expansion and human freedom.

To take one example of this from higher education, Luisa Deprez and Sandra Butler's (2001) study considers issues of access to higher education, an issue I also explore in more detail in the next chapter and return to in Part 3. They explore the issue of low-income women in the USA securing access to higher education under welfare reform measures, and use the capability approach to draw attention to developing the capabilities of people by increasing the choices available to them. They therefore argue that education 'is a major source of women's empowerment, shaping not only the destiny of the educated individual but enabling her to help others in a meaningful way' (2001: 2). It facilitates women's economic participation through meaningful, stable and adequately paid work, their independence and their ability to do things in the future. In particular they argue, higher education 'is crucial for families who are poor' (2001: 6), offering a way out of low paid work, or chronic unemployment. Their research considers the Parents as Scholars programme at the University of Maine, which provides welfare recipients with access to post-secondary and higher education. A survey of participants in 1999 affirmed the positive correlation between higher education, well-being, empowerment, and enhanced relationships with children. Students who completed the survey reported increased self-esteem and confidence and strengthened self-respect – we might describe these as capabilities. Respondents reported having been introduced to new ideas, new friends, new ambitions, and new ways of looking at the world – we might describe these also as capabilities. They had hope and aspirations for a better life, such that one might think of higher education as enabling intergenerational promise, as opposed to intergenerational dependence (or failure). In short, low-income women reported that their participation in higher education 'had enabled them to both see and experience a more expansive range of available life choices' (2001: 17), thereby expanding their freedom. To take the comments of just one of the women in the project who said:

> I feel much more self-confident and comfortable. I have new friends and a new social life. I feel like a complete person now that my life has direction and goals. I am much happier and my children are also. I feel smarter and encouraged by the future, I have goals and hope now.
> (quoted in Deprez and Butler, 2001: 14).

This matter of hope and aspiration is very important, as Ghassan Hage (2001) and Arjun Appadurai (2004) have both so eloquently argued.

Resources and diversity

I am suggesting that it is capability that we set out to 'measure' in higher education, rather than how much money each university is allocated or how much is spent on each student, as these do not tell us about how the resources are distributed and to whom. We might think of resources, such as bursaries for students, teaching facilities, books and journals, computers, the staff-student ratio, academic scholarship, and so on as 'capability inputs' (Robeyns, 2005). At issue is the relationship between these resources and the ability of each individual to convert the resources available to her into valued capabilities. Take for example a physically disabled student. She would require greater input of resources to enable her mobility from class to class and her access to the library than an able-bodied student. She might require special support during teaching if she is blind or deaf. A student from a low income family may not be able to afford her own personal computer and will require more of the university IT resource than a better off student. Average spending per student therefore does not tell us how this bundle of resource is converted by each of these students into valued capabilities and functioning. They are certainly important capability inputs, since persons should have access to the resources they need in order to develop valued capabilities and to support their functionings. But such resources in themselves are only a partial picture of quality and well-being in higher education. They are the means but not the ends of well-being, justice or educational development. A more interesting question would be to ask: if our intention was to promote capabilities in higher education, how would we deploy our available financial resources?

Sen's point is that 'equalizing ownership of resources [redistribution] . . . need not equalize the substantive freedoms enjoyed by different persons, since there can be significant variations in the conversion of resources and primary goods into freedoms' (1992: 33). He insists on 'the basic heterogeneity of human beings', such that human diversity is central to and explicit in his approach to equality, not an add-on factor. It is, he argues 'no secondary complication to be ignored, or to be introduced later on; it is a fundamental aspect of our interest in equality' (Sen, 1992: xi). People will differ along (a) a *personal* axis (e.g. gender, age, etc.); (b) along an intersecting external or *environmental* axis (wealth, climate, etc.); and, (c) along an inter-individual or *social* axis which will generate differences in people's ability to convert resources into valued outcomes. Thus we cannot take men's lives, or the lives of able-bodied people, or the lives of white people as the norm for our evaluations. Inequalities of gender, race and disability are included in and fundamental to the space of functionings and capabilities. Such differences affect our ability to convert the resources we have into capabilities to function.

Thus resources (or we might say redistribution) are only a part of the story; what matters is the opportunities each person has to convert their bundle of resources into valued doings and beings. Unequal resources are an issue, and redistribution is necessary but not sufficient for equality of capabilities. We might add to the issue of how diverse individuals are able to convert their bundle of resources, the matter also of the recognition and valuing of such diversity. The equal recognition and valuing of identities in higher education will shape teaching and learning, as I explain in some detail in Chapter 4 and Chapter 5. Robeyns argues, for example, in respect of gender equality that:

> The cultural and non-material social constraints on choice that influence which options a person will choose from her capability set, must also be critically examined. In the capability approach, preference formation, socialization, subtle forms of discrimination, and the impact of social and moral norms are not taken for granted or assumed away but analyzed upfront.
>
> (2003a: 547)

Matters of resources (distribution) and recognition should be integrated for social justice, as Nancy Fraser (1997) has argued. Robeyns (2003a) has developed a convincing critique of Fraser's (1997) argument that theories of distributive justice ignore issues of the recognition of difference, or the recognitional effects of redistributive measures. (For example, a basic income for women would be necessary but not sufficient to address traditional gendered divisions of labour. It would be redistributive without being recognitional.) Robeyns rather argues that the capability approach integrates both. At issue for education is that economic matters are inseparable from matters of culture and society. Are diverse learners not only equally able to convert the same resources into valued educational opportunities, but also recognized socially and subjectively as having equal claims on such resources and opportunities? It would seem, following Robeyns' line of argument, that the capability approach is able to give particular insight to this question for higher education, where both economic inequalities and cultural injustices shape student and teacher identities and hence pedagogical encounters.

Agency

Central to the capability approach are the concepts of 'agency freedom' and 'agency achievement'. Sen is concerned with 'a free and sustainable agency' (1999: 4) as the 'engine' of development. His concept of 'agency freedom' means having the 'freedom [opportunities] to bring about the achievements one values' (1992: 57), to be free to do and achieve our valued goals, whether or not we assess these goals in terms of some external criteria as well. More freedom makes more (agency) alternatives available. Agency achievement refers to a person's success 'in pursuit of the totality of her considered goals and objectives' (1992: 56). Agency is then one's ability to pursue goals that one values and that are important for the life an individual wishes to lead; agency and human flourishing are deeply connected.[2] Effectively there are agency opportunities (freedom) and agency outcomes (achievements) and we evaluate these individually but also interpersonally and in the context of power relations. Put more simply, agency is the ability to exert control over one's life (Biesta *et al.*, 2004). Being an agent involves both the capacity to choose between options (to go to university or to study plumbing, to choose civil engineering rather than biology, to choose private sector work over public sector employment) and being able actually to do what one chooses (for example, studying engineering). Thus agency is an important dimension of human development understood as capability and functioning and we could argue, the key element of advantage in evaluating higher education pedagogies. Sen explains:

> We might wish to know who has how much power to pursue their own goals. We might also have an interest in checking how successful they respectively are in bringing about what they are trying to achieve. We

may have political and ethical views regarding societies in which some people can promote all their ends while others have to face great barriers which they cannot overcome.

(1992: 71)

Because agency is also central to Sen's ideas of the freedom to make choices, a lack of agency or a constrained agency equates to disadvantage – if an individual (or group, see Robeyns, 2003a) faces barriers to genuine choice and a life of reflective choices. In higher education pedagogy this might build from micro-instances in which agency is restricted to form a pattern over time of agency disadvantage. Barnett and Coate suggest that:

> The scribbled note in the margin of an essay can either lift or deflate. One instance of a tutor expressing the view in writing on a student's essay that, 'this has been written very quickly', can lose in a moment the student's self-belief that has just begun to form and be apparent. The self can be quickly lost to view and in the process will disappear any hope of the student coming to engage – with confidence and fortitude – the experiences that are coming her way.
>
> (2005: 147–8).

One might argue that agency is not a fixed state, and that in non-ideal ('real') situations it works dialectically as both freedom and constraint and is dynamically constituted over personal and social histories and time (McNay, 2000; Comim, 2003). This of course has implications for pedagogical practices as Barnett and Coate suggest, so that being more agentic is always then at least a possibility, and should be fostered pedagogically. What is clear is that agency makes a difference to our lives, including our lives in higher education. Nixon (2005) offers the compelling example of Beatie Bryant, a working-class woman in Arnold Wesker's play *Roots*. Although it is not an example from education, it is a deeply educational example:

> Beatie starts to talk, at first using the terms and arguments that Ronnie [her intellectual lover] gave her . . . [but] she begins to discover her own voice. Wesker through his stage directions, intervenes again: 'Suddenly Beatie stops as if listening to herself. She pauses, turns with an ecstatic smile on her face.' Then Beatie speaks: 'D'you hear that? D'you hear it? Did you listen to me? I'm talking . . . I'm not quoting anymore . . . Listen to me someone.' [Wesker again: As though a vision were revealed to her.] Then back to Beatie: 'It does work, it's happening to me, I can feel it's happened, I'm beginning, on my own two feet – I'm beginning . . .'.
>
> (2005: 137)

Nixon (2005: 137) suggests that Beatie in this learning moment has 'achieved a fragile sense of agency'. This is a powerful and moving instance from which formal pedagogy might well learn about how to create the conditions for Beatie to stand on her own two feet so that her higher education contributes to her agency and human capabilities. At stake is the claim supported here that 'the uniquely human capacity to make choices about one's own life' (Barclay, 2003: 24) is a core value for politics and through politics for a just higher education in which our practices do not work to diminish this capacity but expand it and expand it for all, not least marginalized and excluded individuals and groups.

Social arrangements and institutional conditions of possibility

Now, Sen integrates securing and expanding intrapersonal and inter-personal freedoms (individual agency and social arrangements). We should not, he and Dreze (1995) argue, view individuals and their opportunities in isolated terms. Crucially, functionings depend on individual circumstances, the relations a person has with others, and social conditions and contexts within which potential options (freedom) can be achieved. Individual agency (freedom), Sen insists, depends also on social and economic arrangements (e.g. education, health care), and on political and civil rights:

> Individual agency is, ultimately, central to addressing these deprivations [in the world]. On the other hand, the freedom of agency that we individually have is inescapably qualified and constrained by the social, political, and economic opportunities that are available to us. There is a deep complementarity between individual agency and social arrange-ments. It is important to give simultaneous recognition to the centrality of individual freedom and to the force of social influences on the extent and reach of individual freedom. To counter the problems we face, we have to see individual freedom as a social commitment.
>
> (Sen, 1999: xi–xii)

Individual functionings therefore are influenced by a person's relative advantages in society and enhanced by enabling public and policy environ-ments, for example a gender equity or disability discrimination policy. Sen emphasizes that, 'Being free to live the way one would like may be enor-mously helped by the choices of others, and it would be a mistake to think of achievements only in terms of active choice by oneself' (1993: 44). Social opportunities and social norms expand human agency (or diminish it). For example, social norms in non-ideal contexts (everyday, real life) construct disadvantage, even where public resources might be equally distributed. Unterhalter and Brighouse provide this helpful example of 'widening' access to higher education:

> Ann, who belongs to a group that has suffered race and class discrimin-ation, has two daughters. Imagine that it is very difficult for children from this group to complete school, get higher education, and enter secure high paying jobs in the civil service, not because they have fewer resources spent on them, but because their previous marginalisation

from those opportunities has given rise to a culture in which those are not aspired to, and alternative less materially rewarding avenues are valorised. Ann has to battle against these cultural norms . . . generating conflict with her children and her husband and her own marginalisation within her culture. She succeeds, but the real cost to her (and her children) is far greater than that experienced by a mother of similarly talented children from a group with different values.

(2003: 16)

Individual human capabilities and the fostering of these capabilities through social arrangements are then central to a just society. Social structures are the means, however, not the ends of well-being (Robeyns, 2005). The issue is that capabilities do not develop in isolation but relationally. Nussbaum (2000a) tackles the issue of individual capability and social arrangements by her concept of 'combined capabilities'. These comprise our 'internal capabilities', which Nussbaum (2000a: 84) explains as the 'developed states of the individual herself that are, so far as the person herself is concerned, sufficient conditions for the exercise of the requisite functions'. Suitable external conditions will enable the exercise of the function, she explains.

To take an example from education, a student might have the internal capability for voice, but finds herself silenced in a seminar through particular arrangements of power. In other words the conditions constrain the realization of her individual capability. In Nussbaum's conceptualization, this student has the internal capabilities to handle academic work – she has won a university place – but the (external) conditions in the institution for her to enhance their capabilities are missing or constrained. In Sen's formulation, the social arrangements for individual agency are lacking. What is crucially at issue here is that institutions (and here I have in mind higher education organizations particularly, but also other social and political institutions) provide the enabling spaces and conditions for development and learning in the way that individuals cannot do alone. Nussbaum argues that institutions have power beyond that of individuals; it is then plausible to suggest that the responsibility for promoting human capabilities is institutional. Onora O'Neill (1996: 187) similarly explains that principles of justice are embodied both in public institutions and in individual characters. This 'both-and' approach is important, given that institutions are never perfect or 'knave-proof'; it therefore helps she says 'not to have too many knaves around'. She explicates further:

Even when no injury is inflicted, capacities and capabilities for action can still be undermined and eroded in many different ways. . . . Just institutions can aim to avert and mitigate many of the injuries to which characteristic and persistent vulnerabilities lay people open, but cannot generally avert or mitigate activity that exploits individuals' more variable and selective vulnerability.

(1996: 192).

To return to Mann (2001), at least three of her five responses to alienation – those of solidarity, hospitality and redistribution of power – are as much institutional (higher education, the university ethos) as they are pedagogical in their full enactment and sustainability. Pedagogical boundaries are porous, as much institutional as they are the single biology or literature class, as much about the disciplinary knowledge structures as the individual physics lecture, as much about social structures of class, gender, ethnicity as about the individual student. Pedagogy is situated and contextual and educational identities shaped by social and institutional norms.

Is education always an unqualified good?

In the capability approach, education is a matter of substantive freedom. Sen's approach does not allow that education in schools, colleges and universities might not always operate as the unqualified good which he takes it to be (Unterhalter, 2001, 2003b). But as Mann (2001) demonstrates, (higher) education is not always an unqualified good. A lack of a good quality education can be a serious disadvantage, and one which might persist throughout a lifetime. For example, in Gallacher *et al.*'s (2002) study of mature learners in Scotland, they emphasize the continuing negative impact of earlier schooling experiences on people's perceptions of themselves as successful learners. They quote one of their interviewees: 'I had problems with my level of self esteem connected with my past educational experience. The discouraging thing is really inside me. It is this internal stuff that always comes back and beats me up' (2002: 506). A deep sense of failure at school might then reduce the chances of further educational agency and freedom. Capabilities can be diminished as well as enhanced. For Sen (1999), the idea of 'development as freedom' then provides a perspective in which institutional assessment can systematically occur – as individuals we live and function in a world of institutions. The chances we get are influenced by such institutions and how they function according to social norms and practices to support or diminish development. Thus, he (1999: 142) argues, not only do institutions 'contribute to our freedoms, their roles can be sensibly evaluated in the light of their contributions to our freedom'.

This last point was emphasised in a letter to a British newspaper in which Sara Covington wrote:

> I have been following the debate about getting more poor kids off the streets and into universities. I was myself a poor kid who went to a red-brick [élite] university in a year when the number of applicants was at a peak, and I feel part of the debate is missing. Our universities are essentially middle-class institutions. Poor kids have seldom had the 'benefits' of a middle-class upbringing and thus tend to feel like aliens from another planet on entering such institutions. Despite being as well qualified academically as everyone else, I had no idea of what was

expected of me while at university, and always felt everyone else was attending lectures I had missed. I dropped out after a year.

(The Guardian, 12 February 2001)

So Sara was academically talented, she was accepted by a 'good' university, but she left after a year. For higher education there is then the issue around belonging to higher education communities, being marginalized within them, or being excluded altogether, and the contribution of pedagogies to this. As a graduate first-generation student explained, students from 'good' schools at her élite university seemed much more confident, more 'expansive' as she put it, so that in classes 'they seemed to be able to sort of argue and discuss things and I felt like a little thing in the corner' (quoted in Walker, 2001b: 6). Even succeeding at university – gaining a degree – can produce a damaged identity where the experience has been of exclusion. As this same student explained: 'I tell you I wouldn't go there again. I reckon it really messed my head up because of the structure of classes in Britain, the haves and have nots'.

To take a further example, that of women's participation in small group tutorials or seminars at which students are apparently encouraged to put forward their own responses and ideas to curriculum texts, issues or problems. On the one hand there is each woman student's capability to present her own ideas confidently and convincingly; on the other there is the matter of whether she is heard and listened to. This is institutionally mediated and socially and culturally influenced. Pointing to the gendered nature of pedagogy, Paula Rothenberg writes, for example, about her own learning in an undergraduate humanities course in the USA:

> Our discussion sessions met several times a week and were held around large round wooden tables that, we were led to understand, were used to situate students and faculty [lecturers] on the same plane . . . The round tables were designed to undercut the authority that might accrue to a professor based on his position at the front of the traditional classroom. But in spite of these efforts to stimulate intellectual exchanges and undercut authority, the patriarchal relations that characterized the university and formed its character made it clear whose voice had a right to be heard. The male students brought a sense of entitlement with them into the classroom, and women like myself understood that they were lucky to be there at all. While it was true that anyone could offer up any comment they chose, there was a particular style and form which guaranteed that your comments received a respectful hearing and that form and style was gender based. Attending class at the University of Chicago was like entering an all-male club on visiting day – you were always waiting for the bell to ring, signalling that the visit was at an end.
>
> (2000: 77–78)

The point to be emphasized is that pedagogy (or teaching and learning) is not neutral or 'uncontaminated' by the institutional and social context in which it operates but acts as a complicated carrier for relations of power and privilege. Thus agency in pedagogical contexts includes both individual and social dimensions. As bell hooks (1994: 178) writes, reflecting on her own experiences of higher education as a black working class woman at Stanford University: 'Loudness, anger, emotional outbursts, and even something as seemingly innocent as unrestrained laughter were deemed unacceptable, vulgar disruptions of classroom social order. These traits were also associated with being a member of the lower classes'. Or sociologist Beverley Skeggs explaining about her UK university education that:

> My first real recognition that I could be categorised by others as working class happened when I went to university (an upper/middle-class university that often felt more like a finishing school) and I was identified in a seminar group as 'Oh, you must be one of those working class people we hear so much about.' I was absolutely mortified. I knew what this meant – I had been recognised as common, authentic and without much cultural value. The noisy, bolshy, outspoken me was silenced . . . I did not want to be judged and found wanting.
>
> (1997: 130)

As she points out, it is middle-class social norms and members of the middle class who instigate these judgements. Similarly, Louise Morley, commenting autobiographically on her own educational experiences, writes that for working class women 'becoming "educated" is a complex combination of achievement, struggle and betrayal. It means that wherever we are, there are vast reservoirs of experience and insights we must not speak' (1997: 114). The point here is that these students were constrained in exercising their reasoned agency, and for their full capability development the sources of unfreedom – social and institutional – should be removed (Sen, 1999).

Adapted preferences

Given the problematic of unequal valuing and recognition noted above, Nussbaum (2000a) points to the difficulty with 'adapted preferences'. People adapt their preferences and subjective well-being or choices according to what they think is possible for them, and formal education plays its part in this identity formation. For example: the young woman who comes to believe she is 'rubbish' at school work will rule herself out of further study; or the working class boy who is told higher education 'is not for people like us'; or the high-achieving female university student who is not encouraged to pursue postgraduate work; or the middle class child who is disposed to want higher education because this is what middle class children do (see Ball *et al.*, 2000a and Archer *et al.*, 2003 on student 'choice'). As Nussbaum further explains, our subjective preferences and choices are shaped and informed or deformed by society and public policy. Unequal social and political circumstances (both in matters of redistribution and recognition) lead to unequal chances and unequal capacities to choose. These external (material as well as cultural) circumstances 'affect the inner lives of people: what they hope for, what they love, what thcy fcar, as well as what they are able to do' (Nussbaum, 2000a: 31). Although not describing higher education, Sen captures the problem succinctly when he writes that:

> The destitute thrown into beggary, the vulnerable landless labourer precariously surviving at the end of subsistence, the over-worked domestic servant working around the clock, the subdued and subjugated housewife reconciled to her role and her fate, all tend to come to terms with their respective predicaments.
>
> (Sen, 1985: 15, quoted in Comim, 2003: 7)

I return to this issue in chapters 3 and 5 in the context of how we come to identify valued capabilities for ourselves where those selves are caught up in adapted preferences which we may not recognise as being against our own best interests, always adjusting our expectations to our chances.

Beyond rights

Finally, a brief word about the language of rights, which provides an important claim to justice. The capability approach both supports a human rights discourse but also goes beyond it in demanding that we ensure people's capabilities and functioning. For example, not just the right to equal opportunities for students in higher education, but also the capability to function as participants in equal opportunity educational processes and outcomes. For example, the right to higher education is of course important and hard won historically by women, but we need also to ask about the capabilities of women to access, participate and succeed in higher education, in other words to ask both about their right to a higher education and their capability to be educated and to lead a life they have reason to value (Sen 1992, 1999; Dreze and Sen 1995; Nussbaum, 2003a). We might ask similar questions about working class students, about disabled students, about mature students, and about minority ethnic students. Universities in the UK now have policies that ensure student and staff rights to equal opportunities free from discrimination or harassment on the basis of sex, race or disability but these formal rights need to be implemented and secured in practice, and for my purposes, implemented pedagogically.

Basil Bernstein (2000: 6) significantly links education, democracy and 'pedagogic rights'. He argues for three interrelated pedagogic rights: the right to individual enhancement involving 'the right to the means of critical understanding and new possibilities' (2000: 6) as the condition for confidence, without which, he argues, it is difficult to act. The second right, 'is the right to be included, socially, intellectually, culturally and personally' (2000: 7). The third is the right to participate and shape outcomes. Again, this pedagogic version of rights requires a matching capability if they are to be secured. At issue are Sen's (2002) opportunity and process capabilities, the opportunity capability (capability to be educated) and process capability (capability to participate in education) of education and how their development points to personal and interpersonal advantage. We might agree that Bernstein's three pedagogic rights are norms for equality and quality in higher education and justice for all students. The advantage of this rights discourse is that we would need then to pay attention to any causes of the marginalization, or alienation, or disengagement, or constrained capability of students, and the power relations that perpetuate these (as Mann points to). We might then use pedagogic rights to challenge these realities and the obligations and responsibilities necessary to support shifts in the causes of such marginalization (Pettit and Wheeler, 2005). What a capability perspective then adds, is the argument that higher education falls short of its own equality goals unless the capabilities necessary for these rights have been effectively achieved (see Nussbaum, 2003a). In other words, if we agree to the pedagogic right of individual enhancement, we need to develop the associated capabilities, such as confidence in learning, that secure this right to each student.

Summing up

The capability approach foregrounds human development, agency, well-being and freedom. It offers a compelling counterweight to neoliberal human capital interpretations and practices of higher education as only for economic productivity and employment. It places human capabilities in the 'space' of evaluation so that our evidence for what is to count as 'justice' is evidence about our human capabilities. Educational quality and well-being is assessed in terms of a person's valuable capabilities and functionings – beings and doings. It leads us to ask questions such as: Are valued capabilities distributed fairly in and through higher education? Do some people get more opportunities to convert their resources into capabilities than others? Which capabilities matter most in higher education for developing agency and autonomy for educational opportunities and life choices? In short, it means taking up the 'crucial' importance Sen allocates to education in the formation and use of human capabilities. It further takes up Sen's (1992) core question, 'Equality of what?' As he explains, all egalitarian theories that have stood the test of time pose the issue of equality of something, for example of income, or welfare levels, or rights and liberties, or access to equivalent learning opportunities. He argues therefore that the choice of the evaluative space in which to assess equality determines what equality we prioritise. For Sen, 'equality of what' is answered by 'equality of human capabilities'. In other words, when we evaluate how well we are doing in achieving equality and equity in educational arrangements, it is to people's capabilities that we turn.

At this point, the advantages of the capability approach as a framework for a criterion of justice in higher education are: (i) that higher education is seen to have both intrinsic and instrumental value; (ii) it addresses both recognition of diverse identitics and rcdistribution of resources in achieving valued ways of living and being; (iii) it foregrounds agency as a measure of individual dis/advantage in and through higher education; (iv) it locates individual agency and social and institutional arrangements on the same plane; and, (v) it focuses on the capabilities needed to achieve educational/pedagogical rights.

For higher education we then need to ask (a) what the valuable capabilities (sets of abilities to achieve) are and (b) how valuable are they? In doing so we need further to focus on our underlying values and concerns through which we distinguish and select which functionings are valuable and which less so, or even trivial. The following chapter takes up this issue of selecting capabilities, while also further expanding on the matter of subjective preference formation.

Notes

1 For those interested in the wider literature on the capability approach and human development, a good place to start is the website of the Human Development and Capability Association based at Harvard University (www.fas.harvard.edu/~freedoms), where a wide range of resources can be accessed, including useful papers from training sessions at conferences and work in progress. Additionally the papers from the first two international conferences on the Capability Approach are archived on the website of the Capability and Sustainability Centre at St Edmunds College, University of Cambridge (www.st-edmunds.cam.ac.uk/csc/index.html). The journal *Feminist Economics* devoted a special issue to Sen's work in 2003. Also see the *Journal of Human Development* and the edited collection *The Quality of Life* by Nussbaum and Sen (1993). For work in education which explores the capability approach in relation particularly to John Rawls' (2001) 'primary social goods' (basic rights and liberties, freedom of movement and choice of occupation, powers and prerogatives of offices and positions of authority and responsibility, income and wealth and the social bases of self respect) see Elaine Unterhalter and Harry Brighouse (2003) and Ingrid Robeyns (2004). Robeyns (2003a) has also written an interesting critique of Nancy Fraser's argument that distributive theories of justice overlook issues of recognition.

2 It is important to point out that Sen (1992) links agency freedom and agency achievement with well-being and argues that agency achievement may not always be guided by one's own well-being. For example, a student might decide to join a solidarity fast for political prisoners and thereby reduce her physical well-being. A young doctor might decide to work for a period of time with Médecins Sans Frontières out of her commitments to the suffering of the poor but in doing so endanger her own well-being by working in strife-torn countries. Thus agency and well-being, Sen argues, are distinguishable but thoroughly interdependent. Our choices (agency) are not always guided by the pursuit of our own well-being. We make judgements about which options are important, or more important.

3

What are We Distributing?

> But there is no democratic society that does not take education – the
> French term *formation* is the argument in a word – with utmost serious-
> ness, and none that does not contend with the prospect of educative
> soul making.
>
> (Kwame Anthony Appiah, *The Ethics of Identity*, 2005: 199)

Given that education is so significant in Sen's thinking about development,
rationality and freedom, what exactly is it that we are distributing in higher
education? The previous chapter noted that the distribution of resources is
necessary but not sufficient for full human development for each and every
person. If we are instead distributing capability, can we point more specifically to what this is? Furthermore, can we identify which capabilities matter for
the full development of our students, and for what it means to be an educated person in the twenty-first century? At issue here is whether or not we
think it important to give content to our notion of capability (freedom) in
and through higher education; whether we wish to give content to what
counts as *education* in universities; and whether we wish to give some substantive content to the development of rationality. Is it sufficient to focus on a
deliberative process about what counts as learning and higher education and
ignore the outcome (which might take the form of a situated list)?

Higher education is understood in my argument to be a capability in itself;
having higher education expands social and educational opportunities, and
develops rational choices and freedom to choose a valued life. But higher
education is also made up of a number of separate but intersecting and
overlapping constitutive capabilities, for example, 'knowledge'. My focus in
this chapter is therefore to make progress towards selecting a list of constitutive capabilities. But there is an important debate to be engaged first. It has
two aspects. The first is whether such lists undermine democratic participation and choices (see Nussbaum 2000a and 2003a; Sen 1992, 2004; Sen *et al*
(2003)). The second is whether specifying a list of valuable capabilities that
count for social (and educational) justice impose directly or indirectly a

particular notion of the good life – that one way of life (for example, a secular life) is better than any other and a comprehensive view of what has value in human life. Bringing thcsc two aspects of the argument together would be to ask whether there is a case to be made for the specificity of a (higher) education list for particular purposes, and what might constitute such a case. The point of concentrating on the production of a list is (i) to focus the capability approach both on the specificity of education and of higher edu-cation – what it means to be educated – in what is an expansive human development paradigm; (ii) to develop an argument for pedagogy which fosters capabilities and equality; and, (iii) effectively to test the usefulness and application of the capability approach and the key ideas sketched in the last chapter.

This chapter therefore takes up the debate on whether or how to select capabilities, in this case for pedagogical purposes and goals in higher educa-tion. However, I would not want to cast the debate in terms of *either* deliber-ation *or* a list, but rather to suggest that the best possible situation is to find a way to combine both. Where a best possible situation is difficult, there is still a role, I believe, for outlining a theoretical approach (an ideal-theoretical list) for scrutiny and further work, and as a way to insert capabilities into the higher education debate. Obioma Nnaemeka (2003: 358) reminds us that theory 'plays a central role in helping to scrutinize, decipher, and name the everyday, even as the practice of everyday informs theory making'. We need to have in mind who theorizing is for, even as we recognize its need to be informed by practice and people in the world. Theoretical engagements might work to diffuse privilege and not only to reinforce it. The idea is to promote thinking about positive practical alternatives to what currently is in higher education, and to harness ideas to this end.

Now, Carol O'Byrne (2004) makes a number of useful points about the specificity of higher education. She notes that higher education is not universally accessible, nor by its nature is its provision at the direct front line of poverty reduction (as basic literacy, shelter, clean water and so on are). Students in higher education can be assumed to have satisfied their basic needs, and to have attained at least minimal levels of well-being. The focus is then on more complex capability attainments beyond a basic threshold. Higher education is also currently voluntary, it is part of post-compulsory education, and students for whatever diverse reasons have chosen to be there and one might assume ascribe some value to higher education whether instrumental, intrinsic, or both. Nonetheless, higher education may, and arguably should, contribute indirectly to general social well-being.

For example, in South Africa all medical students on graduation are required to undertake a 'Zuma year' under a policy implemented by the former Minister of Health, Dr Nkosana Dlamini-Zuma, which requires them to spend a year working in rural areas with poor communities before they are fully certificated as doctors. Similarly, alleviating poverty requires the input from a number of university-trained personnel, such as engineers, town planners and medical researchers, who might choose public service of different kinds. Higher education might contribute to social well-being even during the years of student study. Recently Dave Eggers (2004: 1) has argued that universities should consider instituting a public service requirement for graduation, arguing that just as parents need to foster a reading habit in their children so universities need 'to create in their students a lifelong commitment to volunteering even a few hours a month'. He argues that university students are at a point in their lives when exposure to service with non-profit organizations and the people they serve 'would have a profound effect on them' (2004: 2). In short, argues Eggers, higher education concentrates on giving students intellectual tools but largely ignores how they might contribute to the world. The novelist Ben Okri (2003: 20) reminds us that, 'All students ought to be practical dreamers. Universities ought not only to turn out students for the various spheres of business, science, the arts, the running of the economy, management and information technology skills, but people who as human beings enrich the life of the planet'. At issue is that we should not underestimate the role of higher education in both developed and developing counties (even though it might at first sight appear to be a 'luxury' in the latter compared to the urgency of poverty alleviation). As I noted in Chapter 1, higher education offers maps, tools and resources (Colby *et al.*, 2003), as a foundation for later life.

Selecting capabilities

How then do we identify which capabilities in higher education are valuable? Which capabilities are important if we want to evaluate agency and flourishing, both at the core of the approach? The first stage in my argument is to consider in more detail whether it is helpful to generate a list of education capabilities, which in the first instance might need to be ideal-theoretical. Or should we leave the matter open to democratic communication and participation, bearing in mind Sen's injunction against 'one predetermined canonical list of capabilities, chosen by theorists without any general social discussion or public reasoning' (2004a: 77)?

Given the specificity of education and of higher education, and taking Brighouse's (forthcoming) 'moderate perfectionist' stance, I therefore now work towards a provisional, revisable selection of human capabilities to provide general guidance for pedagogical practice. I set out to demonstrate an argument and method rather than to produce a canonical list of universals. Indeed, we should be careful not to collapse the matter of selecting capabilities for a specific situation (higher education) with the idea of a list of universals. In my view addressing the specificity of higher education by producing a list enables us to evaluate what it is we are distributing in higher education, and to check how well we are doing. In short, we should assess education interventions according to the effects on things people value and have reason to value. We need then to ask (a) how is this higher education; and (b) in our context how does higher education contribute to human capabilities?

Sen's participation approach

Sen (1992, 1999, 2002, 2004a) has consistently argued for the importance of public participation and dialogue in arriving at valued capabilities for specific situations and contexts. His capability approach is deliberately incomplete; he does not seek a complete ordering of non-negotiable options. Incompleteness is fundamental to his approach, and pragmatic. He does not stipulate which capabilities should count, nor how different capabilities should be combined into an overall indicator of well-being and quality of life. For him a 'workable solution' is possible without complete social unanimity being achieved. He argues that all the members of any collective or society 'should be able to be active in the decisions regarding what to preserve and what to let go' (1999: 242). There is a real social justice need, Sen (1999: 242) says, 'for people to be able to take part in these social decisions if they so choose'. The process of public discussion is crucial, so that the public as much as the individual is seen to be an active participant in change; citizens whose voices counts.

In Sen's model of deliberation, a dialogical democratic process encourages open and public debate, discussion and dispute around proposals for development, or development priorities, in order to arrive at a collective and reasoned determination of what are the best policies and capabilities. Those affected by any policy or practices should be the ones to decide on what will count as valuable capabilities. Opportunities are also 'influenced by the exercise of people's freedoms, through the liberty to participate in social choice and in the making of public decisions' (Sen, 1999: 5). Sen is therefore quite critical of the idea that 'pure theory' can substitute for the 'reach of democracy', or that a list of capabilities could be produced irrespective of what the public (or publics) understand and value. He argues strongly that to insist on 'a fixed forever list of capabilities would deny the possibility of progress in social understanding' (2004a: 80). This emphasis on participation in turn, however, makes capabilities of literacy, and conditions of a free and accessible media, and of having reasonable chances of participating important. Because Sen is concerned as much with the process – who is making the choice – by which we arrive at an outcome as the outcome itself, this must also then mean paying attention to theories of deliberative democracy, theories of power, and theories of voice and participation.

To translate this into a higher education example, that of developing a capability-based policy for teaching and learning in a university, those affected by the policy – lecturers, students, support staff, for example – should be participants and agents. They would collectively decide on the selection of relevant capabilities, and the institutional conditions should support such participation. Given current hard times in higher education, the radical reach of such ideas becomes apparent – and exciting as an alternative discourse for change and development. Freedom, for Sen (and one might argue following in a tradition, even if not made explicit in Sen, of educators such as John Dewey and Paolo Freire), is concerned as much with processes of decision making as the opportunities to achieve valued outcomes. In other words, we make development and freedom by *doing* development and freedom. Thus a list of capabilities cannot simply be pre-specified without public consultation. Freedom is intrinsically important 'in making us free to choose something we may or may not actually choose' (Sen, 1999: 292). Moreover, Sen argues that a space for justice or fairness does exist in the human mind and that 'basic ideas of justice are not alien to social beings'. At issue is making 'systematic, cogent and effective use of the general [moral] concerns that people have' (1999: 262). Sen is committed to the idea of 'reasoned social progress' based in our shared humanity. He therefore presents individual freedom as a social commitment, arguably framed in an optimistic development discourse (see Seddon, 2003). In other words, change and improvement is possible, and participation and dialogue are key constituents of such change. Even if we produce a 'rough and ready' list of capabilities for a particular purpose (such as higher education pedagogy) it is still the case, Sen (2004a: 80) argues, that 'public discussion and reasoning can lead to a better understanding of the role, reach and significance of particular capabilities'.

Nussbaum's universal list approach

Nussbaum (2000a) has a somewhat different view of the idea of a capabilities list. She argues for a Marxian/Aristotelian conception of truly human functioning as 'the proper function of government' which requires that it 'make available to each and every member of the community the basic necessary conditions of the capability to choose and live a fully human good life, with respect to each of the major human functions included in that fully good life' (1993: 265). She has produced, and robustly defends (for example, see Nussbaum, 2003a), a universal, cross-cultural list of central capabilities for human flourishing and a life of dignity because, she (1998: 314) points out, 'we need to have some idea of what we are distributing, and we need to agree that these things are good'. Her response has been to develop a definite universal list of ten central human capabilities (see Chapter 5), all of which would need to be present for a fully human good life (see Nussbaum, 1998, 2000a, 2003a). Nussbaum therefore seeks to give a specific content to capabilities, arguing that Sen's reluctance to make commitments about what capabilities a society ought centrally to pursue means that guidance in thinking about social justice is too limited. Her list, she claims, is tentative and revisable, but together the ten capabilities constitute 'a minimum account of social justice' (2003a: 40). Nussbaum refutes the charge (for example in Barclay, 2003) that her list prescribes a comprehensive notion of the good (Nussbaum, 2003b: 27), that is, that it promotes individual autonomy as foundational to a good life. Nussbaum does not therefore argue that to reject individual autonomy, for example by choosing a non-autonomous religious life, would be to reject a truly 'good life'. Nussbaum points to her emphasis on capability rather than functioning and her support for an 'overlapping consensus' for the content of her list among people 'holding a wide range of divergent reasonable comprehensive doctrines' (2000a: 5).

Nussbaum's list has been criticized (see, for example, Spelman, 2000; Alkire, 2002; Walker, 2002a; Okin 2003; Robeyns 2003b; and for her defence Nussbaum, 2003a), in so far as we do not know through what, if any, process of public debate the list was produced, whose voices are heard, how it is to be revised and by whom. Nussbaum (2000a, 2003b, 2004) argues that her list is humble, open-ended and revisable, although it is not clear who will revise it. For Sen (2004a) her list is 'canonical' and this is problematic for him; as noted above he leaves his framework deliberately vague, because of the importance for him of communities deciding what capabilities count as valuable. Now, Sen (2004a: 79) has also said that he is not opposed to lists per se, 'so long as we understand what we are doing (and in particular that we are getting a list for a particular reason, related to a particular assessment, evaluation or critique)'. But he would argue that to specify a single list of capabilities is to change the capability approach into a capability theory, whereas he intends it to operate as a general framework for making normative assessments about quality of life.

Arguments towards an ideal-theoretical higher education list

Taking the two positions together, I would argue that there is a valid case for a list, but this should be for a particular purpose, or evaluation, or critique; it should not be fixed or canonical, it should not be hierarchically ordered, and it should in some way include participation and dialogue. The idea is for higher education communities participatively to produce their own flexible, revisable and general list, but *not* one definite list of higher education capabilities for all contexts. This case turns in part as well on the argument about the *specificity* of education as a part of human development. A working list provides a content to what we take to count as 'higher education'. It addresses the case for a theoretical understanding of the human good and hence of the 'education good' (Deneulin, 2005). Does anything count as higher education and higher learning? If not, how do we judge who in higher education is lacking capabilities central to higher learning? Should we then produce a list, or lists, in order to indicate the content to a norm of social justice in higher education? Should we try to work out what such higher education might look like and then consider how practice and reality accords with our view of justice (Nussbaum, 2003a)? At issue, is that if we raise questions about equality in higher education, we need some idea of what we take to count as 'higher education'. As Nussbaum (2003a) robustly states, unless we do this we end up saying that we are for justice but that any old conception of justice is all right with us. Robeyns (2003b: 35) points out that while at some abstract philosophical or theoretical level one might argue that all valuable capabilities matter, 'this is no option for second-best [non-ideal] theorizing or for applications'. For example, considering people as subjects – agents – of their own lives is central in the capability approach. Sen (1999: 18) emphasizes 'the ability of people to help themselves and to influence the world'. A lack of agency or a constrained agency equates to disadvantage. We might then begin to argue that it is equally key in higher education and we ought then to decide what capabilities support agency development. From here we would then need to consider the ways in which higher education as an opportunity and as a process develops agency in learners. We might also begin to argue that if agency is being disabled in some way, then higher education is diminished and its quality under-mined. On this basis the matter of 'which capabilities?' and flowing from this, what we are distributing in higher education as/for justice needs to be addressed.

I therefore set out to produce an ideal-theoretical list, that is, it has not been generated through public participation and is limited in this respect, but making it public is to invite participatory dialogue. But I wish first to address three matters.

1. Functioning, not just capability

The first is the matter of developing capability only or also functioning. An emphasis on the latter would begin to prescribe how someone should lead their lives, and hence to have an implicit view of the good life. To take an everyday example of some concern in UK universities at present, that of a student 'binge' drinking culture. Fostering capability might involve a university educating students in responsible alcohol consumption, and about alcoholism. Functioning would then be left up to the students who may or may not choose to drink heavily knowing the health and safety risks. Sen (1992, 1999) promotes the notion of autonomous persons and sees human well-being as founded in the capability of the individual agent to critically reflect and make worthwhile life choices from the alternatives available to the individual person. The point is that capability, he would argue, equips us to determine our own major goals in life and we should not prescribe for adults how they should live. Nussbaum (2000a, 2003b), as noted earlier, favours the Rawlsian idea of an 'overlapping consensus' among people who hold a plurality of conceptions of the good life. She argues that her list of central (generic) human capabilities is grounded in a view of 'truly human functioning' (2000a: 76) but does not seek to prescribe 'any particular metaphysical view of the world, any particular comprehensive ethical or religious view, or even any particular view of the person or human nature' (2000a: 76).[1] Nussbaum claims that her list is Socratic, and invites us to ponder what is implicit in the notion of human dignity and of a life in accordance with it'. We might translate this into asking, what is implicit in our notion of human dignity and which pedagogies in higher education are in accordance with it?

The point under debate here is that both Sen and Nussbaum claim not to prescribe a specific conception of the good. To advocate functioning, they would argue, would be to advocate living life in particular way. For example, not only to have the capability for autonomy but to function as an autonomous human being, thereby ruling out any choice of a non-autonomous life as valid and rationally chosen.

Now, Harry Brighouse (2000: 65) argues that autonomy should be a fundamental value in the design of educational policy; and 'all children should have realistic opportunity to become autonomous adults', because autonomy 'enhances dramatically the ability of individuals to identify [for themselves] and live lives that are worth living' (2000: 88). Social justice, he says, 'requires that each individual have significant opportunities to live a life which is good' (2000: 68). It then also follows that children need to develop a sense of what it means to live well, to be able to compare different ways of life, and to choose a good life for themselves. This in turn involves fostering the capability for critical reflection on one's own goals and values as 'an essential part of living well' (2000: 67). Children should, argues Brighouse, learn how to access truth, weigh up evidence, investigate and think about their decisions and so learn a 'critical attention' to the options available to them. However, Brighouse is careful to distinguish between an autonomy-facilitating and an autonomy-promoting education:

> The argument claims that equipping people with the skills needed rationally to reflect on alternative choices about how to live is a crucial component of providing them with substantive freedom and real opportunities, by enabling them to make better rather than worse choices about how to live their lives. The [autonomy-facilitating] education does not try to ensure students employ autonomy in their lives, any more than Latin classes are aimed at ensuring that students employ Latin in their lives. Rather it enables them to live autonomously should they wish to.
>
> (2000: 80)

In other words, he too leaves open for adults to make their own choices.

Brighouse's idea of an autonomy-facilitating education is similar to one of the central capabilities on Nussbaum's (2000a: 78) list, that of 'practical reason', which she describes as 'being able to form a conception of the good and to engage in critical reflection about the planning of one's life'. She insists that in the interests of democracy and tolerance in society, children 'not be held hostage to a single conception [of the good life]' (2003b: 42) but that they are exposed to other ways of living. Her concern is that they should have the capability to critically reflect and plan, and if they so choose to opt for a non-autonomous life in which this capability will not be exercised (functioning), for example, if a life in a traditional religious community is chosen. She argues that the state has no business telling adults 'that they are not leading worthwhile lives'. Thus adults might choose to live non-autonomously. Nussbaum is therefore clear 'that we shoot for capabilities, and those alone [i.e. not for functionings]. Citizens must be left free to determine their own course after that' (2000a: 87). For Nussbaum this includes choosing a non-autonomous life, in other words she does not claim that personal autonomy is the only valuable style of life. For her a life lacking the *capability* of practical reason 'is not a life in accordance with human dignity' (2003b: 39), but this is different from insisting that we should all function in this way. But, to this we must add, and emphasize, that to judge or describe someone as autonomous 'is to make the normative judgement that their reasons for choosing as they did were neither trivial nor bad, but both good and important ones' (Kerr, 2002: 3). Autonomous persons 'have the general powers of deliberation, reason and judgement required to conduct one's own affairs and to participate in the state' (Kerr, 2002: 4). Moreover, we might also argue that we cannot claim to want to foster autonomy in education on the one hand, and then say what kind of life pupils and students must then choose, on the other. This is helpfully illustrated by turning to Arendt (1977: 177) again. She is concerned to emphasize the unpredictability of the future and the possibilities of change, renewal and a better life through human agency coupled to educational processes in which no one 'strikes from their [students'] hands their chance of undertaking something new, something foreseen by no one'.

Nussbaum has in mind adult choice in her discussions of practical reason (autonomy); she is clear that in the case of children we require that they remain in compulsory education (schooling) until they have developed the capabilities that are important in enabling them to have genuine and valued choices, for example to exit from a traditional community. She concedes that we cannot develop a mature adult capability without having some practice of it. She states therefore that 'education in critical thinking and debate is a compelling state interest', and that children should be taught to develop (learn) these capabilities in debating complex and controversial social and moral issues. They can, she says, always reject the teaching later. She has pointed out with respect to children, that we might need to promote a relevant capability 'by requiring the functioning that nourishes it' (2000a: 91). In other words, functioning is required for further development of a capability. She gives the example of requiring children, especially girls, to spend time in play, story-telling and art activities as a way to promote the general capability of 'play' for the girls and the women they will become. In other words they need to do it (function) in order to develop the mature capability. Nussbaum suggests that 'the more crucial a function is to attaining and maintaining other capabilities, the more entitled we may be to promote actual functioning in some cases, within limits set by an appropriate respect for citizen's choices' (2000a: 92). Thus, with regard to the education capability of practical reason (autonomy) we might argue that it is crucial for children and young adults to practise critical thinking and reflection, and for us to evaluate their functioning in these areas in order that they might develop and enhance this capability through education and higher education.

We similarly need information to tell us when an absence of functioning means absence of the capabilities we have agreed are valuable in our higher education context. Assume that we think respect to be an important capability. If a young man harasses a young woman at university, or if students denigrate or insult a student from a different ethnic group or religion, we can deduce from their actions (functioning) that they lack the capability of respect. To take another example, where a lecturer presents him or herself as *the* authority about some aspect of the subject being studied and is dismissive of student attempts to discuss or offer alternative views, it becomes difficult for undergraduate students to see themselves as co-constructors of knowledge, or to find and use a critical voice in relation to this knowledge. They might then become mimics, ventriloquists and reproducers of what they feel the lecturer wants from them, or as Mann (2001) might argue, alienated. But to be alienated is to not have the capability for agency and confidence. There is then a somewhat complicated articulation of capability, functioning, action and direct information for judgements about how well we are doing educationally. At issue, as Nussbaum points out, is when 'requiring functioning is the only way to ensure the presence of a capability' (2000a: 93). Robeyns (2003b) adds a further dimension to the argument when she considers group inequalities (in her case gender inequalities). She argues that 'inequality in achieved functioning implies inequality in capabilities, except if one can give a plausible reason why one group would systematically choose different functionings from the same capability set' (2003b: 84). For example, if women were to avoid certain subjects at university, or to attain fewer first class passes than men in examinations, we would need to raise questions about the capability sets of the women and men, unless we wished to claim that it was reasonable to assume that there were good reasons for their choices and achievements.

But higher education is again a somewhat different case from that of schools, and universities are not simply extensions of schools, or more of the same. Students enter higher education as young adults and as mature learners. We make assumptions that they have achieved a measure of autonomy already, albeit that this may be uneven. Jonathan (2001) argues that in post-compulsory education, the state no longer has the fiduciary duty to determine the interests of young people, nor to prescribe particular moral, social or cultural experiences. Thus, she writes (2001: 49), 'As adults, students are deemed the arbiters of their own interests – and of their values and cultural allegiances'. We therefore might need to rethink the relationship between capability and functioning for university students. We might offer students the opportunity to acquire knowledge and to use higher order analytical thinking, but we cannot in higher education demand that they function as knowledgeable and analytical persons. We cannot prescribe any particular version of the good life, and all versions are possible. We might enable the capability for compassionate citizenship through teaching English literature, or history, or sociology, or philosophy, but we cannot compel our students to function as compassionate citizens. We might provide young people with opportunities for the capability of voice, or for emotions and imagination, but we cannot demand that they function as imaginative, emotionally aware persons. On the other hand, in higher education as in schools, practices and achievements will both shape students' experiences of higher education and as the letter from Sara Covington (Chapter 2) suggests, will affect later choices and opportunities. What we do in higher education will have future impacts on choices and opportunities. On this basis we might argue that functioning and not just capability is as much a matter in higher education with adult students as it is for young learners in schools.

The fuzziness of the boundary between only promoting capability in higher education, or also paying attention to functioning should be addressed, if only because capability as noted in the previous chapter is counter-factual and difficult to measure or evaluate. Thus functioning is often taken as a proxy measure of capability (Gaspar and Van Staveren, 2003; Robeyns, 2005). The point is that in education we probably do have to evaluate functioning but we need to do this in the context of not prescribing to students the choices they make about their own lives, and respecting a plurality of conceptions of the good life within a democratic society. Nussbaum puts this well:

> Of course I support mandatory functioning for children; that may be the only way to develop an adult capability. Even where adults are concerned, we may feel that some of the capabilities are so crucial to the development or maintenance of all the others that we are sometimes justified in promoting functioning rather than simply capability, within limits set by an appropriate concern for liberty.
>
> (2000b: 130)

We need to be clear that respecting a plurality of conceptions of the good life is not the same as endorsing all versions of the good life, and this has clear pedagogical implications. For example, a member of a far right group might well endorse racism as part of their version of the good life and the good society, and this would support racist teaching and the dissemination of racist knowledge. But in Sen and Nussbaum's conceptualization, to be racist or to enhance racism is not to enhance capability because human freedom is being diminished not expanded, human dignity is being compromised, and human flourishing for each and every person is being denied. Jonathan (2001) points out that no teaching, including teaching in universities, can be neutral. Decisions are made as to what counts as knowledge, what counts as ways of knowing, and how knowledge is to be taught and evaluated, and all these decisions will be inflected by personal and academic values and the institutional context. At issue is that curriculum and higher education is purposeful and values-based. To take just one recent example from the Harvard University Faculty of Arts and Sciences curriculum review (Harvard, 2004), there is a clear statement of purpose regarding that a liberal undergraduate education in the arts and sciences at Harvard is intended 'to educate our students to be reflective, disciplined and independent thinkers' (2004: 1). More specifically, Harvard's aim is:

> To provide students with the knowledge, skills and habits of mind to enable them to enjoy a lifetime of learning and to adapt to changing circumstances. We seek to educate students to be independent, knowledgeable, rigorous and creative thinkers, with a sense of social responsibility, so that they may lead productive lives in national and global communities.
>
> (2004: 6)

This then has particular curricular and pedagogical implications, which are explored in detail in the review. Jonathan (2001: 49) emphasizes that 'while explicit values teaching is not an option for higher education, value learning is inevitable'. What higher education in its teaching and learning practices can then do, she says, is provide 'the conditions that make desired outcomes possible and to avoid scenarios which actively work against them' (2001: 52).

2. Worthwhileness, values and the good

Now this does not necessarily make the case for an ideal-theoretical education list, although it does begin to call into question strong notions that anything goes, or that any list will do in the sphere even of higher education. Even if we are only indirectly promoting some idea of worthwhileness and values through higher education, can we think of justice in higher education without some notion of the good, or rather what is lacking? (Deneulin, 2004). Paul Ricoeur argues that we cannot conceive of justice without a view on what is lacking (the good):

> It is from a complaint that we penetrate the domain of the just and unjust. The sense of injustice is not only more striking, but also more adequate than a sense of justice; because justice is often what is lacking and injustice is what is reigning, and humans have a clearer vision of what is lacking in human relationships than the right way of organizing them. It is the injustice that sets thought in motion.
>
> (1991: 177)[2]

Nussbaum (2000a) and Sen (1992, 1999) as we have seen, do not prescribe to people what lives they must lead, in other words how they use their capability, or that they must choose this good life rather than that, although they do make the case for everyone signing up to human rights and broadly shared democratic principles such as 'liberty' and 'equality'. For his part, as noted earlier, Sen places great store by processes of political participation by the communities affected in decisions about freedom and capability and is vague about the content of freedom beyond seeing it as inherently positive. Yet this arguably still leaves freedom underspecified, so that Gaspar and Van Staveren (2003) argue for the contribution also of values like democracy, respect and friendship, while Nussbaum (2003a) points out that not all freedoms are good when divorced from wise judgement. For example, a lecturer might have the freedom to humiliate a student in the classroom or in a graduate supervision meeting, but it is questionable whether this is an educational use of the lecturer's freedom. A group of young women might have the freedom to exclude someone who is working class from their middle class peer group, but this is again a questionable exercise of their freedom. The educational issue is how through higher education we develop the capability to make good judgements, but also what we then take to be 'good' rather than not so good or even bad judgements.

This brings us back to the issue of justice in education and a conception of the good. As Harry Brighouse and Adam Swift (2003) point out, education is not a neutral activity; it always embodies a view about what is good in human life, otherwise it might 'seem vapid, even pointless' (2003: 367). For this reason, like notions of the public good, it is contested. Education, Brighouse and Swift say, is unavoidably normative and requires 'a clear and defensible conception of social justice' in the content and distribution of educational opportunities, and for our purposes here, the distribution of capabilities. In other words, not all versions of the 'educational good life' are equally worthwhile and we might argue that education should inform children and young people about what are thought to be worthwhile alternatives (Winch, 2004). In turn this suggests that in schools and universities a somewhat weaker form of autonomy would operate in education but still within the frame of human capabilities and what this implies for *both* rationality *and* freedom, and human flourishing. Moreover, whatever the age of the students, all education aims to change students in some positive, life-enhancing way. Otherwise we could say, it is not 'education' (but it may be training or indoctrination).

We might argue that not all rival conceptions of education contribute to human flourishing; 'bantu education' in apartheid South Africa is a case in which something called 'education' was designed to stifle choice and freedom. We might also not wish to describe as education a process which encourages prejudice against a racial group, which tolerates or encourages the sexual harassment of girls and women, which belittles some religious beliefs or practices, or which treats those with mental disabilities as less than human. Moreover, while Sen (1992: 41) might leave the capability approach deliberately under-specified, nonetheless he does also say that 'individuals should have substantial well-being freedom', that is freedoms to achieve well-being, and this will point to how good a deal each person has in society. We could also argue that there are different conceptions of education compatible with human flourishing. But 'education' which contributes to *un*freedoms (gender exclusion, marginalization, hatred or prejudice) would be deeply incompatible with the capability approach in which education is understood as enhancing agency, well-being and freedom. The key issue here is to be clear that education enhances humanity, agency and well-being by 'making one's life richer with the opportunity of reflective choice' for a life of 'genuine choices with serious options' (Sen, 1992: 41). In short, what we call 'education' should not diminish lives.

What I am approaching here is the notion that some kind of 'list' of education capabilities may well be appropriate. It would constitute a kind of 'moderate perfectionism' suggested by Brighouse (forthcoming). Here I am with Nussbaum (2000a, 2003a) when she argues for a thick vague theory of the good, where for my purposes the good in higher education would be selected capabilities, but the vagueness would involve leaving the detail to be worked out in specific contexts by the participants. Framing such a list and deciding what to include is no easy matter. But, Nussbaum says, we have to face this question if we are to take the capabilities approach forward and make it productive for thinking about matters of social justice. For my purposes we need then to have an account of central higher education capabilities 'even if we know that this account will always be contested and remade' (Nussbaum, 2003a: 56). The argument is helped by Richard Arneson's (2000: 37) discussion of perfectionism and politics in which he raises the questions as to whether 'there are things that are good in themselves for an individual independently of her desire and attitudes towards them?' Are there education capabilities which we might argue are objectively good for an individual's educational development? Is it good in itself for a student to acquire the capability of respect, or critical knowledge, for example? Which capabilities enable students in higher education to become 'good choosers' (Arneson, 2000: 45)? A 'moderate perfectionism' is then arguably the way forward.

3. Adapted preferences and choices

I now wish to revisit the interlocking nature of the individual, individual choices and social and institutional arrangements outlined in the previous chapter as a matter of how we get to be 'good choosers' and how higher education ought to contribute to this. People adapt their (subjective) preferences, I briefly explained in Chapter 2, according to what they think is possible for them. It seems that our choices are deeply shaped by the structure of opportunities available to us through what the sociologist Pierre Bourdieu (1977: 72) describes as our habitus, 'systems of durable, transposable dispositions, structured structures predisposed to function as structuring structures'. Rao and Walton apply his ideas by arguing that:

A disadvantaged group can view its status within the hierarchy as correct and appropriate. By positioning a group within the social hierarchy, consequently, culture affects their sense of the possible. For those at the high end of the hierarchy, it provides the means to maintain their high position, whereas for those at the low end it can limit aspirations, create discrimination, and block mobility.

(2004: 15)

Bourdieu (2003) explains that 'structure tames chance', so that our antici-pated future (our 'forthcoming') is imagined in relation to our present and past, rather like the schools of which students say 'you wouldn't succeed if you went there'. Our future aspirations turn on what we take to be possible for ourselves. Individual lives come to accommodate their social chances in the 'game' of life, which is not fair:

> Without being strictly speaking rigged, the competition resembles a handicap race that has lasted for generations or games in which each player has the positive or negative score of all those who have preceded him, that is the cumulated scores of all his ancestors. And they should be compared to games in which the players progressively accumulate posi-tive or negative profits and therefore a more or less great capital which, together with the tendencies (to prudence, daring etc) inherent in their habitus and partly linked to the volume of their capital, orient their playing strategies.

(Bourdieu, 2003: 74)

We adjust our hopes to our probabilities, even if these are not in our best interests. We are, says Bourdieu, 'taught by the order of things', and we learn through daily encounters with education and the workplace what is the thing for us to do. This takes additional force from the iterative nature of learning. Learning is seldom linear, more often it is recursive, it involves us adapting what we already know (our past-present) and who we are now to new (present-future) conditions of possibility.

But adapted preferences notwithstanding, there is also no simple deterministic reproduction of social relations of privilege by the education system. There is always room for a struggle over the meaning of the world, the possibility of resistance and a rupturing of the habitus, as feminist work on agency (McNay, 2000; Hughes, 2002; McLeod, 2003) argues. For example, if family life offers one narrative of the future and university friends offer cultural scripts for a new identity of 'university student'. Such work seeks to address the reproductive effects of structure and habitus without ascribing undue weight to agency by holding both agency and structure in simultaneous relation. The point for the capability approach, as Flavio Comim (2003) argues, capabilities need not be fixed. Rather, he explains (2003: 7), because individuals 'seem to be adaptive beings, their agency is constantly evolving towards adaptation to forms of freedom and unfreedom'.

Over time our agency might be enhanced or eroded, our preferences adapted more or less towards our flourishing. For example, failing one assignment might be distressing, continuing to fail over the course of an undergraduate degree is likely to cumulatively reduce confidence and agency. Not finding a voice in seminars becomes cumulatively more difficult over time. On the other hand having success and enjoyment in one's university work in turn builds confidence. For example, Rosie, a first generation student then in her second year of studying English literature, spoke about completing her essay on Shakespeare. She talked about really enjoying going to the library and 'churning through the critics' and reading the Shakespeare, 'taking it to pieces and seeing the professor and seeing what he said about it and writing it and having to think really, really hard, what do I actually believe and having to order my ideas. I really enjoyed writing it and I got a first for it as well' (quoted in Walker, 2006: forthcoming). Comim (2003) usefully develops the idea of 'capability paths' as a dynamic way of capturing change over time. Thus we could argue that the capability approach offers us a means to analyse change over time, recognizing the interaction of the social and the individual and the social constraints on choice such that we might adapt to a given habitus, but also making the possibility for agency central and important.

The relevance for the debate about developing a list or not, is that we need a degree of care in how we interpret people's choices, which they happen to express at some moment in time. In societies where women's education is not valued as much as that of men, women accept the restrictions on their higher education opportunities. Nussbaum (1998: 316) explains that, 'in the absence of education and the knowledge of alternatives women [students] themselves will frequently endorse a conception of the good in which they remain subordinated and ill-educated'. She goes on to ask a critical question: 'have we dealt with them more justly here, when we allow them their alleged freedom to choose in accordance with the conception of the good they have than we would if we insisted on compulsory primary and secondary education for women?' For example, what if a group of students were unable to recognize or have the frameworks to understand Mann's (2001) alienating practices in higher education? It is not impossible that outside of an ideal-theoretical list for higher education, they might not see particular practices and obstacles to their developing capabilities as problematic. Indeed, following Nussbaum's argument, they may not even identify certain capabilities as of value to themselves.

Therefore, in Nussbaum's view 'too quick a flight from the question of the good' (1998: 316) ensures that dominant ideas in a society will continue to prevail, even if these are not in the best interests of all its members, nor ones which all would endorse 'on fullest reflection'. We have to pay attention to the way processes of education lead to preference formation and deformation, working class women, for example, wanting to leave school early, or disabled students accepting their exclusion from access to and full participation in higher education. The student who is consistently told that she is 'thick', whether by parents or friends or teachers (or all of these) will rule herself out of getting more education unless and until some kind of second chance opens up for her as a mature learner. We might also point to the compelling account of student alienation provided by Mann (2001) – students who come to blame themselves for the effects of institutional power relations, for the disappointments in their learning, for their inability to learn the rules of the game of higher education, for their increasing reluctance to speak out in tutorials and seminars. A student lacking in confidence but with high academic ability might come to adapt to her second-class performance as the best she can do, rather than challenging the poor quality of tutor support. This of course is not to deny the capability for agency in resisting such conditions, or for refusing to assimilate to the institution's values but it is to argue that many working class students and many young women are silenced and see their choices as 'freely' chosen, for example adopting a middle class demeanour and values as the norm (hooks, 1994). As a matter of ethical higher education and pedagogy we cannot simply assume that all students will have or come to have the resilience that enables them to develop, notwithstanding unfavourable circumstances.

Models of social justice in (higher) education

At this point it is useful to rehearse again the different ways in which we might set about evaluating educational development as another way of reviewing the arguments made in this chapter and Chapter 2 for establishing 'equality of what?' Unterhalter (2004a) identifies four key ways in which we might do this. Her focus is on gender equality in schooling, but we might easily apply her framework more broadly to 'measure' pedagogical processes and learning achievements and outcomes. The first of her four approaches is termed 'resourcist' and involves providing resources for educational equality. In higher education we might interpret this as the numbers of lecturers and the lecturer-student ratio, the number of student places, additional funds for widening participation and disabled students, library funding, external grant income and so on. Or we could take a simple per capita amount available from state resources to each university. We might then compare across universities in Britain in terms of student outcomes, say the number of first class degrees or the number of students in employment six months after graduation. Equality according to this measure would mean equality of resources. It could of course mean an equal levelling down of resources, as has happened in Britain over the last two decades. The limitation of the resourcist approach is that asking how much higher education, or perhaps more specifically how much each university, or even each department, has in the way of resources, does not tell us how much each member of that university or department can command in the way of those resources. But we might nonetheless want to include resources as important capability inputs in a capability metric.

Unterhalter's second approach is termed 'structuralist' and looks at how gender (and we could argue other forms of difference in higher education, such as race, disability, age, social class) is produced through social relations, institutions and cultural forms of understanding. Equality here would involve removing discriminatory measures, for example through a gender mainstreaming policy in higher education, or through the mechanisms of anti-discriminatory legislation applied to higher education as is the case in Britain. Unterhalter points out that education is understood by a structuralist approach to include what happens in schools and universities, and also a wider set of social, political, economic (labour market) and cultural relationships. The usefulness of a structuralist approach is the way it makes clear that curriculum and pedagogy reproduce social norms. The work of Bourdieu (Bourdieu and Passeron, 1977) on French higher education argued that working class students were less successful because the curriculum was structurally biased in favour of middle class knowledge, values and experiences, or 'cultural capital', and this in turn was played out in relationships between lecturers and students and among students. Social structures shape pedagogy and student experiences of success or marginalization. These structures would need to be changed for equality in education to be possible.

Unterhalter's third approach is termed 'post structuralist' and this approach evaluates gender equality and other forms of difference as a process of identity formation and performance (doing gender). Unterhalter suggests that such an approach foregrounds concerns with discourse, power and identities through which processes of engagement and disengagement in formal education might be negotiated. The value of this approach is in showing the complexities and ambiguities of identity processes and the myriad working of power so that at different times the same student may experience herself as successful and at other times as failing or struggling. Identity formation is hybrid, multiple, and shifting. Oppression and resistance are then more complicated such that education might be both reproductive and transformative. It opens a space for agency, albeit circumscribed by structures. Equality would require changing structures but also changing the conditions for agency in education.

All three approaches to equality point to important dimensions of development – to resources, to structures of opportunity in society and to identity formation. In education, social justice is generally considered along these three dimensions (Griffiths, 1998; Gewirtz, 1998; Power and Gewirtz, 2001; Cribb and Gewirtz, 2003; Vincent, 2003). Drawing on the work of Iris Young (1990), Vincent (2003) explains the limits of a distributive model of justice in education because this obscures cultural complexity and difference and diversity. She suggest that Young's five faces of oppression (exploitation, marginalization, powerlessness, cultural imperialism and violence) combines distributive and cultural dimensions of justice. Cribb and Gewirtz (2003) explain that distributive justice would include both economic justice and the distribution of cultural and social resources. Following Fraser (1997), cultural injustice is defined to include cultural domination, non-recognition and misrecognition of identities and disrespect. Fraser's (1998:

36) concern with 'participatory parity', that is whether one can participate on a par with others in social life, further points to associational justice, to processes of public participation and dialogue across inequalities of power, and to how subordinated groups are involved in decision making (also see Young, 2000). Fraser (1998: 30) argues that 'Justice requires social arrangements that permit all (adult) members of society to interact with one another as peers'. One can see how all three aspects of justice might play out in higher education and pedagogies – economic justice through redistribution of resources, opportunities and employment possibilities; recognitional justice through acknowledging and respecting diversity; and associational justice as due attention to participatory processes.

Unterhalter's resourcist and structural models are broadly equivalent to distributive justice, her post structuralist model broadly equivalent to recognitional and associational justice. In other words, these approaches appear compatible and all point to the plural dimensions of social justice in education and all offer useful lenses to explore higher education. What, if anything, then makes the capability approach of foregrounding 'valuable beings and doings' (Unterhalter's fourth model) a better model of justice in education? How the capability approach accommodates both distributive and recognitional justice is well explained by Robeyns (2003a). Resources are part of the story 'but what ultimately counts is the real opportunities people have to be and to do . . . the real or effective (in contrast to formal) opportunities people have to lead a life they have reason to value', she explains (2003a: 545). Recognitional matters are taken up through attention to cultural diversity, preference formation and social constraints on choice. Associational justice is addressed through Sen's deep concern with public participation in identifying and valuing capabilities, although one could argue that he is weak on a theorization of unequal power. Sen's associational justice would include all people in higher education and not see only some, for example the physically disabled, as special non-normal cases. What emerges from Robeyn's account and Unterhalter's four models is that the capability approach offers a model of justice in education at least as good as the three-dimensional model widely accepted in education.

But more than this, the capability approach is good additionally in the following three ways. The first is in its emphasis on beings and doings, it operationalizes Cribb and Gewirtz's (2003) theoretical argument for social justice as both action and evaluation and their emphasis that we are all responsible for fostering social justice in education in our everyday relations with others. Through attention to fostering capability in and through education, the capability approach indicates a practice as well as a theory along the three key elements of social justice in education: redistribution, recognition of diversity and identities, and participation. Secondly, more than the other approaches it applies to all people, so that disabled people in higher education for example, would not be regarded as 'special cases' (Robeyns, 2003a; Terzi, 2003; Unterhalter, 2003a). Thirdly, it is able to encompass multiple aspects of change so that in higher education, for example, pragmatic and messy development projects which lie some way from theoretical reflections on criteria of justice can be evaluated and change recognized and understood (Robeyns, 2003a; and see Seddon, 2003). In this way it is an optimistic development discourse. Put simply, then, the capability approach offers 'the most promising normative framework we have at present' (Robeyns, 2003a: 551), and more specifically for my purposes, suggests a criterion of justice in higher education.

Developing a list

Given the specificity of education and of higher education, and taking Brighouse's (forthcoming) 'moderate perfectionist' stance, I now develop a provisional, revisable list of human capabilities to provide general guidance for pedagogical practice. I set out to demonstrate an argument and method rather than to produce a list of universals. In my view producing a list enables us to evaluate what it is we are distributing in higher education, and how well we are doing. In short, we should assess education interventions according to the effects on things people value and have reason to value. We need then to ask how higher education *in our context* contributes to human capabilities.

An outline of higher education capabilities has already begun to emerge from this and the previous chapter. The capability approach attaches great importance to agency, to genuine reflective choice, and to ethical and informed citizens. We might therefore argue that education should foster agency and the capabilities constitutive of agency. We might say that fostering the capability of personal autonomy to choose from alternative ways of living is educational and part of the process of education. Sen ascribes an instrumental role to education for realizing economic opportunities, which we might provisionally describe as a capability for paid work. Sen and Nussbaum both attach importance to the relations a person has with others, to the social role of education and generally to the capability to be a full participant in society, so a capability for social relations is arguably important. In the context of higher education such social relations might take the form of interested, approachable lecturers and care from and to peers in learning arrangements and friendships. Diversity is central to Sen's approach so recognizing and valuing difference, we might argue, matters in higher education.

I approach this more concretely by working towards a selection of capabilities in the form of a provisional list, not over-specified or too prescriptive. This selection of capabilities, or 'dimensions' (Alkire, 2001), is multi-dimensional, and this is of crucial importance, because learning is itself multi-dimensional. Each dimension supports the others and all are important. Thus in developing and implementing higher education pedagogies it would not be sufficient to select one capability from the list and work only to develop or enhance that single dimension, for example 'knowledge'. As Alkire (2001: 8) suggests, dimensions of development are like the 'primary colours' of values, and 'an infinite range of shades can be made from our primary colours and not every painting . . . uses all or most shades. But, if for example, all yellow hues were entirely missing, then my understanding of colour would be consistently skewed'. To translate this into educational terms, if learning experiences consistently excluded, say, 'respect' then our framework of learning and educational development would be limited, impoverished in some way.

In the field of education as a practical and theoretical activity, we further need some kind of dialectical iteration of selected capabilities and contexts of practice and action, reviewing our selection in the light of practice but also in the light of new theoretical claims. In other words, any selection would require recurrent empirical testing and participatory discussion (Alkire, 2001). Lists are useful 'not if they are universally acclaimed but if they are effectively used to confront the many challenges of their generation' (Alkire, 2001: 19). The following three chapters now turn to a method for selecting a draft list of higher education capabilities, including empirical voices.

Notes

1 But see Linda Barclay's (2003) critique of Nussbaum's claim to political rather than comprehensive liberalism, and Nussbaum's (2003a) rejoinder. Also see Richard Arneson's (2000) argument for perfectionism and Nussbaum's (2000b) rejoinder. She does admit to being a perfectionist in a sense in that she holds that without certain capabilities such as sociability and practical reason only a subhuman type of functioning is available. She nonetheless claims to support 'respect for the diversity of persons and their comprehensive conceptions' (2000b: 129).
2 I am indebted to Severine Deneulin for bringing this issue and this quote to my attention.

Part 3

Pedagogy and Capabilities

4
Learning and Capabilities

Learning is a human process which has an effect on those undertaking it.
(Ronald Barnett, *Learning to Effect*, 1992: 4)

This first applied chapter takes up capabilities and learning, contributing to the points made about pedagogy in this section of the book, and drawing on student voice data. The idea is to begin with a kind of quasi-anthropological exercise (see Comim, 2004) to find out what capabilities selected students value. There is no claim made that these voices are either representative or comprehensive, simply that we need to take student voices into account in selecting capabilities.

There is a central concern with knowledge in this chapter, and how this is mediated through curriculum and pedagogy, with particular effects for student learning. While the next chapter explores broader framing conditions of teaching methods, learner support and friendship for non-traditional students' learning, the emphasis here is on the distribution of capability for intellectual quality. The issue here is how subject knowledge is made available to and acquired by diverse students.

Because learning ought to be the point of teacher communication of subject knowledge to students, that students understand, that they are changed in some way, this chapter further notes the vital importance of teaching in the pedagogical relationship. It is teachers who make key communicative decisions and implement teaching methods, even if not always under conditions of their own choosing. Thus teaching is certainly part of the story told here, although the balance of focus is on students and their learning. Nonetheless, I want to acknowledge the human complexity of the task that we describe as teaching and the central importance teachers have in creating opportunities for learning, including generating passion and imagination and producing equity (but also too, for potentially reproducing inequities and restricting learning horizons). In a recent paper Gloria Dall'Alba and Robin Barnacle (2004) advocate learning as an ontological (being) project as much as an epistemological (knowledge and knowing) project. They cite

Heidegger's argument that teaching is more difficult than learning 'because what teaching calls for is this: to let learn' (Heidegger, 1968: 15, quoted in Dall'Alba and Barnacle, 2004: 13). Taking up this claim in relation to contemporary teaching in universities, they argue for an integration of knowing, acting and being in students and teachers. Letting learn, they say 'requires creatively enacting situations as pedagogical, being open to, and engaging with the issues encountered, being sensitive to students' needs, and promoting self awareness and reflective practice, with the risks and opportunities that this entails' (2004: 13).

In different ways the teaching which supports the learning described in this chapter might be framed as a version of critical pedagogy in the awareness of power relations in society on the part of the lecturers, and the need to understand wider social conditions and structures, while at the same time enabling learners' human agency. Moreover, there are genuine attempts by teachers to recognize their own power, to give learners a voice, and to open spaces for critical participatory dialogues. At the same time, these teachers may well not describe their work using the language of critical pedagogy, and it would therefore be inappropriate to push too far in the direction of labelling their work in this way. Even if lecturers' own positionality and values are not closely explored in this chapter, I would argue that in the examples I provide a teaching narrative of scholarly expertise, creativity, openness, responsiveness, commitment to learning, and reflexivity in mediating subject knowledge acquisition underpins the teaching approaches adopted.

This chapter is not about claims to the 'right' pedagogy, or perfect transformation in learner understanding and agency. It is not about teaching for closure in learning. The excitement of pedagogy and pedagogical practices lies in the complexity, contradictions and the process of struggle towards transformative practices, which can be aspired to, but never perfectly achieved (Bathmaker and Avis, 2005). Teaching and learning in this view will 'always be uneven and fractured' (Bathmaker and Avis, 2005: 16). Narratives of real life in university classrooms, where teaching and learning are committed and serious, do not seek to create best practice models or to make generic claims for what works. Rather I tell specific and situated stories that point, I hope, to potentially useful principles for ways of working. My empirical examples are illustrative only and drawn from the humanities and social sciences so that in all kinds of ways they are skewed in terms of the broad spectrum of teaching and subjects found in universities. But this is not the point. Rather I am trying to develop an argument which draws on empirical examples to explore the robustness of the capability approach. The idea is to maximize the contribution higher education pedagogies might make to the broader purposes of higher education's contribution to democratic and cultural life.

Learning

Building from these points, and in order to explain more about what I take to be learning, I draw on Stewart Ranson's (1998) attractive theory of learning for its resonance with ideas of being, knowing and acting, and for multi-dimensional agency achievement, which is so central to the capability approach. Ranson suggests the following. Firstly, that learning is multi-layered, that is, it proceeds from developing one's understanding of pieces of knowledge (for example, of British imperialism in Africa), to a growing awareness of our own personhood (how do I relate to these historical events? what do they mean for me?), and then to a capacity to shape the world (how do I act on this knowledge?). Learning is fundamentally a positive and hopeful process of deepening understanding:

> Learning helps us to discover why things are as they are and how they might become different. Such understanding grows from processes of reflection that reveal the connections between things which had been previously unrecognised or opaque to us. To understand is more significant than to know what. To learn how to explain things or events is to be able to grasp the principles which underlie and make sense of their working, and thus to enable us to recognize their occurrence on some future occasion even though the surface characteristics appear to be different.
>
> (1998: 18)

Learning to understand ourselves, he argues, is not separate or a lucky spin-off gain, but central to the quality of our intellectual development (our gaining of knowledge) and thinking.

Ranson secondly argues that the quality of our thinking necessarily reflects both our emotional maturity and our cognitive powers. Nussbaum (2001: 1) has also argued that our emotions are 'a part and parcel of the system of ethical reasoning'. A person may care deeply about reason in the form of ideas and arguments, but have little sense of generous connection to or care for the world and real life problems. Jane Martin (2000: 132) suggests that we do not do well in trying to address the world's problems 'under the direction of people who try hard to be rational . . . but do not know how to sustain human relationships or respond directly to human needs, indeed, do not even see the value of trying to do so'. Feelings and reason are not separate but inextricably related, and educating our emotions, taking emotions into account in producing and disseminating knowledge ought then to be a higher education capability. Nussbaum (2001: 1) explains: 'If emotions are suffused with intelligence and discernment, and if they contain in themselves an awareness of value or importance, they cannot, for example, easily be sidelined in accounts of ethical judgements'. For example, compassion in learning about historical accounts of genocide or imperial oppression enables us to respond to human suffering. Or we might argue that awareness of ethical debates in science is part of the quality of scientific thinking. This is arguably important in higher education where we educate lawyers, teachers, doctors, social workers, engineers, research scientists, and so on. At stake, as Dall'Alba and Barnacle (2004) would argue, is not just the acquisition of knowledge in higher education, but ways of being and knowing.

Ranson's third 'learning layer' turns on the role of agency in learning. He writes that learning 'leads into action and grows out of the experience which action enables: it creates the capacity for *self-creation*' (1998: 19, his emphasis). Learning then takes form 'through our agency in the world' (1998: 19). In language similar to that of the capability approach, Ranson continues, saying that the deeper significance of learning lies 'through its forming of our powers and capacities, in our unfolding agency' (1998: 19). The central purpose of learning then, is that the skills and knowledge we acquire enable the development of 'our distinctive agency as human beings' (1998: 19). Echoing Comim (2003), Ranson points out that learning is a temporal process of becoming over a lifetime, and hence our attempts to evaluate learning at one point in time (say at the end of a module) are necessarily partial. Thus when we speak to students about their learning or their views of our teaching we need to be careful not to construct a singular truth or narrative, or to squeeze these voices into a one-dimensional model of practice, or decontextualized teaching tips. Ranson (1998) further affirms that learning is deeply social; we develop our understanding with and through others.

Like Nussbaum (1997, see Chapter 1), Ranson suggests that the idea of the 'examined life' is key to our developing practical reason, by which he means deepening our sense of our own agency through reflective deliberation in and on a plurality of perspectives, and judgement which leads to action. Indeed, in the current climate of fear and polarization across religions and cultures globally, Nussbaum (2004: 2) argues for a liberal higher education which undoes 'baneful and complacent habits of mind, producing global citizens who can think well about the problems of today's world'. She emphasizes the importance of linking liberal education and a deep, inclusive citizenship and of rich human connections in creating a critical public culture 'through an emphasis on analytical thinking, argumentation and active participation in debate' (2004: 2). Through public debate with others, we develop our critical knowledge standards which we apply to our own perspective and that of others, under conditions of openness and exposure to a plurality of perspectives.

To be sure, says Richard Bates (2005), global means multi-cultural and this in turn means wrestling with differences across and within cultures. This leads Bates (2005: 105) towards a foundational value for democratic life: 'the freedom to build a personal life which respects an equal freedom for others to do likewise'. Here he has in mind a position which takes a stand against both uncontrolled markets and also cultural traditions which are oppressive for some or all community members. His position, as he acknowledges, is similar to and draws from Sen's (1999) advocacy of the development of human capabilities to support greater personal freedom to live a worthwhile life. For

Bates, the educational question turns on developing a global curriculum (of which pedagogy would be a component part) based on twin foundations:

> Firstly, the foundation of intercultural communication and understanding upon which, in the recognition of the other we can form a democratic social structure that celebrates human rather than market values. Secondly, the building of those capabilities that Sen advocates as a foundation for participating in social development in ways that enhance individual freedom to live a valued way of life.
>
> (2005: 106)

Like Bates's global curriculum, Nussbaum's idea of cosmopolitanism (citizens of a world community) encourages Arendtian imaginative 'visiting' across differences of gender, race and class, and cultures and an 'other-oriented curriculum' (Papastephanou, 2002: 71). But Nussbaum's cosmopolitanism is not without critics. Papastephanou (2002) cautions against a definable human nature (the common humanity Nussbaum emphasizes) because we risk, she argues, then measuring cultures according to how near or far they approach this definition. Echoing Young's (2000) and Boler's (1999) concerns, Papastephanou suggests that the notion of a narrative imagination risks an uncritical kind of empathy which simply deprives the other of her voice by speaking for her, and which claims to 'know' how it feels to be handicapped, or working class, or black, or poor, and so on. Moreover, she criticizes Nussbaum for arguing for cosmopolitanism only through Western voices. Papastephanou points to the slippage in Nussbaum between cosmopolitanism and globalization, and suggest that this rests on a 'naïve political optimism' (2002: 76) which risks erasure of the morally deficient aspects of globalisation and 'historically accomplished exploitation or hierarchical structures of production' (2002: 77). It might happen, for example, that cross-cultural understanding might simply enable those with more power to dominate those with less. By contrast, Bates's (2005: 96) global curriculum recognizes a multiplicity of voices and knowledges, citing Foucault's 'insurrection of subjugated knowledges', and the reclaiming that Bates advocates of marginalized knowledge as 'central to any concept of a socially just curriculum' (2005: 96).

The idea of cosmopolitanism as an unequivocally attractive idea has also been taken up by Fazal Rizvi (2005) in his study of international students from China and India who study in Australia. He identifies contrasting conceptions of cosmopolitanism which are either consumerist or critical, where the former describes international students who participate in an economic exchange and are most concerned with its economic possibilities for their own lives. This is rather different from a critical and self-aware cosmopolitanism which incorporates teaching about leading productive moral lives, as much as about building effective professional careers in the global economy. The latter is for cosmopolitan solidarity, not economic exploitation. I have briefly noted Rizvi's challenging critique to make the point that a pedagogy of/for the examined life is far from straightforward. One might also add that

Nussbaum (2004) overstates the potential for a Western liberal higher education to change the world. That education can and does make a difference informs our commitments as educators; that it makes all the difference is however in some considerable doubt (Lingard, 2005).

Part of the difficulty is what one does pedagogically when there is real cultural conflict in university classrooms. The hard educational question is still how a capability for sensitive, subtle, responsible and accountable judgement and an enlarged and imaginative mentality is fostered in students. Moreover, Ranson (1998) points out that deep learning of this kind takes effort and time and requires an agentic motivation to learn, grounded in the view that such learning has a purpose. But this learning disposition, he suggests, turns on a confident sense of self, or put another way, a secure identity as a capable learner. And because learning is social, this identity is socially made in relationships of caring and responsibility with and to others, so that 'reflective interdependence' (1998: 22) is the condition for autonomy, agency and mutuality in learning.

All this constitutes a challenging higher education, and is generally harder to realize in practice, notwithstanding the stories Nussbaum (1997) offers in *Cultivating Humanity*. Maria Misra's (2005: 58) account of her own teaching of the historical topic of European Imperialism at the University of Oxford in England offers a compelling example of the nature of this challenge. Misra recounts a 'renaissance in student politics' in her history seminars but also suggests that this 'repoliticisation' engenders problems of its own. From being a 'sleepy backwater' of a subject she now finds, under contemporary political and social conditions in which Empire is either glorified or critically dissected, that her classes have become the site of passionate debates on European imperialism. As a teacher, she says, she finds herself acting as a kind of umpire for heated student exchanges and 'fiercely conflicting views'. She writes:

> In a recent class on the economic development of India under the Raj, one student was angered at criticism of the British and launched into a heartfelt and pungent defence of pax Britannia. This produced derisive titters from the rest of the class. Another class dealing with the role of colonial governments in enforcing subordination of women in Islamic populations became a fraught exchange between the women in the class – one of whom wore the hijab [veil].
>
> (2005: 58)

Difficult as it may be when students speak out on such topics, it may be more disturbing if they do not. Thus as a teacher, Misra is reluctant to avoid politically charged and controversial subjects because, she argues, this is more likely to entrench than challenge prejudices. But nor is she in favour of the ridicule that students sometimes resort to, or unwonted aggression in promoting one's point of view. She does suggest that 'only when views one disapproves of are expressed by people one knows and can empathise with, does toleration and understanding emerge' (2005: 58). In her classes students from a range of political positions have to engage with opinions they would not normally entertain, expressed by fellow students not dissimilar from themselves. 'Students', she says, 'find themselves conceding some of their opponents' points, and something resembling common ground often emerges' (2005: 58). She therefore argues for the importance of higher education not only for its contribution to a knowledge economy, but for its key role in producing tolerance.

Misra gestures towards the importance of a shared spirit of inquiry and a process of recognition under which students come to tolerance – that humiliation, ridicule and aggression are not acceptable in seminars which aspire towards an imaginative plurality. The speaking of some students should not effectively silence others. This returns us to the importance of recognition as a capability, discussed also in Chapter 5 and helpfully elaborated by Rauno Huttunen and Hannu Heikkinen (2004) in Finland. Drawing on Charles Taylor's (1992) theorizing of recognition and Axel Honneth (1995) on the importance of self-confidence, self-respect and self-esteem in human social development, they emphasize Taylor's claim that authentic recognition ('more than polite words') is an essential human need. Processes of learning and identity formation 'are intrinsically connected with the process of recognition', they say (2004: 164). They argue that by receiving recognition from (significant) others, one achieves a confident and positive identity – 'one learns to know oneself and one's special characteristics' (2004: 165). One learns that one 'has the right to exist as the kind of person one is' (2004: 167), and self-esteem then builds through the respect accorded to one's work, whether orally in classes or written in assignments. 'It is essential', they write (2004: 167–8), 'that people [students] are recognised for work through which they express themselves'. Disrespect involves a withholding of recognition, even where the work produced is worthy of such respect. Here one might point to relations of power in classrooms which produce exclusion, whether deliberately intended or not. Failure, then, to receive the necessary social approval in a significant 'value community' (for example, from one's peers and the lecturer in seminars), they suggest, generates 'negative emotional reactions' (165). Huttunen and Heikkinen include two autobiographical examples from their own learning to emphasize their argument. One of these is drawn from university subject teaching and is therefore particularly pertinent for the purposes of this chapter. It is worth quoting in full:

Rauno's story

I was a student of philosophy, then, trying desperately to find my own place. I wanted to show other students and teachers that I was a talented individual capable of writing 'proper philosophy' and presenting creative interpretations. I had already received good grades for previous examination and seminar work, but in this last advanced studies seminar I had invested considerably more passion and energy. I was very much looking forward to it.

Unfortunately, the professor who usually supervised advanced seminars was unable to come that day. Somebody else was to supervise the seminar instead. This substitute supervisor, however, was himself in a situation of a hard struggle for recognition in the department, as he had just received his post after a bitter debate. So, the seminar situation was very tense. Two persons, both powerfully struggling for recognition, were present. The substitute supervisor tried to show that he was worthy of the professor's trust to conduct an advanced seminar although he had not yet presented his doctoral thesis. The student presenting his seminar paper, i.e. myself, wanted to show that he was a valid and talented philosopher.

The tense seminar situation eventually turned into a catastrophe for me. The supervisor had a much better command of the substance of my seminar paper than I did. He revealed the essential and factual errors in my work. All my sophisticated interpretations and innovations went down the drain. The supervisor hammered my seminar paper. He did not have anything positive to say about it, although I had used quarter of an academic year just to prepare for that particular seminar. I acknowledged my defeat. I tried to withdraw with dignity but the supervisor did not even give me an opportunity for that.

I felt humiliated and offended. I even thought of changing my main subject. The fact that I rather admired this department's newcomer made the situation worse. I wanted to make philosophy the same way he did. My paragon became the destroyer of my seminar paper.

(2004: 170–1).

Here we see knowledge, teacher and teaching and the student in a pedagogical relationship, an encounter which leaves both bruised, but which is arguably far more difficult for the student. Moreover the teacher has some responsibility towards enabling Rauno's learning rather than his humiliation and shame. We also see confirmation of Nussbaum's (2001) argument for the integration of the emotional and the cognitive and we see the mutual shaping of both cognitive/intellectual and emotional capabilities at work in this instance of deformed learning. Huttunen and Heikkinen (2004: 172) argue therefore that we need positive 'circles of recognition', infused with reciprocal respect for all members of the circle, a Heideggerian 'being with' so that each learning community 'is guided by something higher than an individual consciousness: by a collectively constructed culture and spirit'.

Student voices and valued capabilities

What we then have is a view of teaching as 'letting learn', and of higher learning as the developing of intellectual capabilities in the acquisition of knowledge and understanding, involving emotions and feeling, learning which is social, recognitional, participatory, reflexive and actively agentic. I now turn to examples of higher education pedagogy to take further these ideas. I explore three teaching and learning examples[1] from humanities teaching (history), social science (management) and professional education (town planning) at three different British universities to illustrate how higher education might foster capabilities which are valued by students. I tease out from my extended discussion with students what has been valuable and important for them. The accounts described here are evidence-informed, but they do not claim to represent the views of all the students on each course, or to represent similar courses. Rather they set out to illustrate how, through students' voices, we might identify valued capabilities in higher education. They therefore further illustrate the method – student voice – of enabling greater participation in identifying valued capabilities, which can then be used to produce a list as proposed in Chapter 6.

1. Humanities education, an example from history

In the first example I consider a third year elective undergraduate module on 'Liberation Wars in Southern Africa'. This is taught over two semesters rather than only one, and led by the same tutor throughout, which enables the tutor and the students to develop a relationship over time to support learning. All the students commented favourably on this. The lecturer responsible for the course is a senior and very experienced university teacher and a highly respected scholar within the field of study. Eight of the 15 students volunteered to be interviewed individually at the end of the course on their experiences of learning and teaching. Interviews lasted about an hour and took place during one week, 12–16 May 2003. (In addition a number of informal conversations took place with the lecturer, and I looked at the course outline, at a selection of student essays, and at the student evaluations of the course.)

The student interviews make it clear that acquisition of knowledge is at the heart of the pedagogical relationship. It bears repeating that we cannot talk about teaching and learning in universities without also talking about knowledge as knowledge and not only knowledge as knowing, or knowledge as skills or competencies. Teaching and learning activities and experiences are negotiated by the lecturer in the light of his specialized knowledge and in the context of who his students are, but such activities are always focused on communicating subject knowledge. Intellectual quality is therefore a core feature of the teaching on the module. It was important to these students to own the knowledge they had acquired, rather than being seen as pale imitators of the professor's knowledge. As Sarah said, 'it's my degree, my study, so it should be my own work', and this is closely tied to asserting their own independent critical voices rather than being told what to think. Michael said that he had 'carved out my own path, my own understanding and analysis'.

But this in turn seems to have been shaped by the ability of the lecturer to open public space for students to explore and assert their own perspectives. Catherine explained how things had worked in their seminars:

> I never got the impression that he [the lecturer] was ruling lots of things out. I mean people would come up with lots of suggestions and ideas and you know, wondering whether this might have happened or whether that was possible and he was always very open about it. I don't think he was ever making things up, but he did seem to say that 'yes it's possible', he seemed like he was thinking about things himself, he wasn't just sitting there.

This then further links to the importance of developing a deep and critical understanding. Catherine continued:

> One of the things that concerned me over the [history] degree is that I'm learning lots of new things and lots of new subjects, but there's not been an opportunity to just think about it in the sense that you have to look at sources more critically and deconstruct them and to think about subjects in a different way really; there hasn't been much opportunity. It wasn't just learning about a new subject in this module, and learning everything there is to know about it and finding out all different opinions. It's been more sort of questioning things and looking at things in more depth which is what I was hoping all the way through [university] would happen.

Such learning is further related to the importance of the plurality of voices in the class, to social relations of respect and recognition from peers and the lecturer, and to the lecturer's skill in 'holding it all together', as David said, 'when people are spilling away . . . from the main focus of the seminar'. This included relationships of non-humiliation and the lecturer not thinking 'oh you're being really stupid' (Sarah). But this positive recognition was also provided by fellow students in the group as David, Sarah and Jenny emphasized. Sarah explained that, 'I never felt that if I wanted to say something it would be laughed at or knocked down or dismissed . . . if you're comfortable and happy in your surroundings you're willing to participate more'. Jenny remarked that working together with another student for the seminars 'really helped because it meant I got to know someone who I worked with a lot throughout the rest of the module'. At issue was the creation of confidence-building in 'positive circles of recognition' and plurality. Catherine valued the development of her own confidence 'to think about questions that are complex' and to raise questions from the outset without feeling she first needed to acquire all the necessary knowledge. Sarah learnt from others in the seminar because 'everybody does have different perspectives' and Catherine felt that, 'If you have everybody who is the same, you're never challenging your [own] ideas . . . you can stay narrow-minded . . . you've got to constantly question your judgements and justify what you think against other people . . . I'd hate to be in a class where everyone was the same

... you'd not really learn anything'. 'Often I would have an idea', said Michael, 'and suddenly somebody would counter it and it would make me think, perhaps even change my understanding of it'. The learning outcome, as Brian explained, is being able 'to make clear and reasoned judgements, and being able to present those judgements coherently'.

Critical knowledge was fostered in this seminar by an empathic engagement, which was rigorous rather than sentimental. The seminar draws on a wealth of video material to enable students to 'be there', to see the people and the place in historical time. The teaching material was intended to stimulate imaginatively entering the lives of others and to respond to these lives. For example, students commented on being deeply moved by the video biography of the Pan African Congress leader, Robert Sobukwe, leader of the well-known South African pass laws protest at Sharpeville in 1960 and subsequently inhumanely imprisoned in solitary confinement. David commented that he had found the video 'quite emotional really'. The incarceration of this intelligent man, 'it was just a waste of a human life especially with what he could have achieved'. Brian was equally impressed by this material and found it 'an amazing and personal and moving account of his life', saying that he felt such life histories are a 'really important part of historical knowledge'. Despite the differences in his life and that of Sobukwe's 'it was very easy to empathise with his frustration with the repression he was experiencing and the agony he went through in prison . . . so you know it sets the mind working as to how horrendous that must be and it really made me think about it'. But he was still clear that the video was one source and that other historical material should be consulted as well. Sarah spoke about watching filmed material on the South African Truth and Reconciliation Commission in which she found person after person recounting deep injustice and pain 'hard to watch' (see, for example, Krog, 1999). It is important she thought not to get 'too emotional' but it is also important she said to empathize with the people she is studying. 'If you're researching', she said, 'you've got to stand back and be objective, but if you're studying people, I think it's important to try and put yourself in their situation'. Michael suggested the need to balance empathy and reason but also emphasized that if you do not have some compassion for the suffering and dignity of others 'then that's not particularly human, is it'.

For these students, the desire to acquire new knowledge was closely related to their motivation, or put another way, their disposition to learn. Students mentioned having a personal interest in the subject, sometimes because of family connections with southern Africa, or early political memories of families boycotting South African goods during the apartheid period, or just a desire to know more about a part of the world they had not hitherto studied. This interest in the subject did motivate the students to work hard. But it is important to note that the initial motivation to undertake this course is then fostered and enhanced by interactions with the lecturer. Sarah explained that the encouragement of the lecturer 'really made me want to work . . . if your teacher is willing to look at things and help you, you're sort of willing to give more back'. Later she comments that even if the subject were 'amazing', 'if the teacher was not interesting or not helpful, then I'm the sort of person who would switch off and not bother'. Arguably we should not underestimate the sheer enjoyment students get from a course well taught, on a subject that interests them. As Kate said, 'I've really enjoyed it, the subject, and the way it was taught. It was so interesting to think about'. Nor should the lecturer's subject expertise be overlooked. As Kate added, 'it was run by someone who, that was his speciality. . . . yeah, it makes a difference'.

Students also valued the interest their lecturer took in their own learning. Thus David said that the lecturer's interest in helping students learn 'makes you want to work harder'. Michael explained that if a teacher is seen to be learning from his students 'that gives you a sense of pride or encouragement within your own work'. Students were supported in individual essay assignments for the seminars by meeting with the lecturer to talk through their planned essay structure and reading, and William recounted coming away, 'feeling far more confident, 'cos he'd generally say something good and positive so you instantly started off on a bit of a high and you wanted to throw ideas at him and he encouraged me to make bold statements . . . so you actually leave feeling that you've got a really good understanding'.

Finally, how did these students relate the course to their own lives in the world? Was this knowledge something of value? Sarah said that she valued looking at other cultures and countries because once she is in the outside world 'you're going to come across people with different views and if you can't take their views on board, then I don't think you'll get very far in life really'. She welcomed having been made 'to look at things more critically' and while she had planned to do volunteer work in Africa before taking the course she now felt she would approach this work less judgementally, more tolerant of other people, other histories and other views. Brian had become more aware through the lens of southern African history of questions about British society, which have led him to question 'how committed a lot of British politicians are to getting involved in changing Africa'. And he had been made aware of his own privileges, and relative safety living in England. Michael felt he would draw on this historical knowledge for the light it shed on the shortcomings of international politics in relation to liberation struggles, which he sees 'as a goal to work towards if we're ever to achieve genuine participation in democratic societies'. For him university education ought to make connections between higher education and the society in which it is embedded, and to take a stand on addressing problems of poverty and apathy within the political process. 'I think there is nothing worse', he said, 'than producing a class or group of apathetic, unconcerned people who have no other interest than purely seeing something as having to get a job done because of their own interests'.

I would argue that the capabilities that students valued, as emerged from their voices in interviews, are: (i) knowledge – critical, understanding and ownership of, and also acting on this knowledge; (ii) a disposition (motivation) to learn; (iii) exposure to a plurality of perspectives; (iv) social relations in the group and in relationship with the lecturer; (v) recognition and respect from peers and the lecturer; (vi) imaginative empathy and emotional engagement with other lives, times and places; and (vii) being 'let learn', that is, being self-directed and independent but within a clear course structure and lecturer support.

2. Social science, an example from management

In my second example, I consider what students value in a module on 'Cross-Cultural Marketing' taught in a department of management. I draw primarily from the focus group discussion interview with seven volunteer students from the 20 on the course. This took place on 30 May 2002 and lasted about two hours. (Other data collected included two in-depth interviews with the lecturer and course materials.) This second year elective module draws students from a number of countries: in 2002 it included students from Germany, France, Japan, Korea, Oman, the USA and English students from diverse ethnic backgrounds. The course sets out to challenge students to think about cross-cultural management practices differently from the more traditional accounts; class sessions are interactive and participatory; and the reading load is both relatively high and demanding. Edward Said's *Orientalism* is the set text for the course. The lecturer describes 'identity' and 'difference' as key tropes. The course presents mainstream management theory but asks students to think about who is constructing this discourse, while the second half of the course offers a post-colonial critique to think about 'how else could the world be' (interview, 15 April 2002). The lecturer aspires to some kind of global curriculum (Bates, 2005) and critical cosmopolitanism (Rizvi, 2005) in that he hopes his students will historicize and challenge their own positions and consider how they might ethically change things for themselves (15 April 2002).

Students indicated the value of having developed a critical understanding, saying they valued: understanding that 'the world is globalising and the world is being brought together' (Philip); 'thinking for ourselves more, and questioning things that we have been taught' (Jasmina); being able 'to look at an article and you think who has written it and why has he written it like that . . . and that counts a lot in our essays [but] no-one has taught me and made me think like that until this course' (Tasneem); and gaining 'political knowledge' in which events current in the world were taken up in class (James). Some students found themselves questioning previous assumptions so that Tasneem said, 'I would never have thought about the position of women in Arab countries; it wouldn't have struck me that this is part of a whole tapestry of gender relations across the globe'. But gaining such critical knowledge is never uncomplicated. These students expect to have to apply their understanding in the business workplace, and not all of them feel this course on marketing will help them much in their working lives. The knowledge is intrinsically valuable but some see little instrumental use for it, which they would also have welcomed.

For some of the students critical knowledge about the subject and their valued learning extended also into reflective self knowledge. For example, three of the students commented on how this new knowledge had or might change their selves, closely relating this to perceptions of difference, while a fourth felt it would not change his sense of self. As this issue of difference and identity was core both to the curriculum and to student experiences and valued learning on the course, the extract of dialogue is quoted at length:

Tasneem: I mean for me, the course did make me think differently because, I mean, one of the main aims of the course was that people, other people are not homogenous, they're very different and you have to appreciate that each individual is unique. But it acts in how you look at other people; people think of themselves as a homogenous group. So me being a Muslim, I would always think that every other Muslim is like me but then Stephen [the lecturer] would say something like 'Islam is practised differently in different countries' and it's true, the same religion is practised very differently in different countries. I suppose the fundamental values are more or less the same, but the way it's practised is different and that influences the way people think as well. So in that sense, yeah, I've learned to be more sceptical and more critical about myself, my religion and where I come from as well.

Johan: I think that's a good point. I think one cannot actually say that one has changed fundamentally; I'd say it's like a gradual thing. You're like starting to not take everything as objective and to start to deconstruct it a bit. However, if it's actually going to affect me later on in work, I don't know. 'Cos like I mean the management discourse has been established to create power in a way, right, and if I'm in a company I will always be benchmarked against other people who use that knowledge without questioning it. If I say 'Well we can't do this other stuff because it'll impact on the people in a bad way', I don't know, it might be difficult for me to sustain my position. I don't know, I mean it's like going into ethics I guess. It's difficult to say how one would behave in the future.

Tasneem: I suppose, but it would help you understand people better I think, like you'd always give them the benefit of the doubt, think that there's more to what they show than what really is there, you know. You don't take things at face value, so it's very good in terms of your relations with people, it's very political in that sense, the course was. It talked about relations of power between people and I suppose in that sense it is useful.

Johan: So did it help you to reduce the stereotypes you have about certain cultures?

Tasneem: To a large extent, yes, it does, yeah, it does. I'm more careful about making generalisations now. I am. I don't know about everyone else.

Katrina: I think what Stephen was getting at most of the time was actually making us more open-minded, like stepping outside from the fixed sets that we're thinking in. Sometimes when he was like very particular about these issues, I thought I'm not that narrow-minded anyway, that's sometimes the impression I had. Not like, that I think that everything that's different from me is like not good or everything that's different for me, I'm afraid of.

Jasmina: I think for me he explained most of the things that I've been confronted with in my life. 'Cos I'm from England but my parents were born in India and I have studied abroad in America and I've been confronted by people who didn't know much about my parents and why they came to England and have been living here and that their children have been brought up in this country. It's hard because, I mean, I'm a British citizen but still I've got my Indian culture and I've got my Muslim culture as well and it's helped me to understand it better, it's helped me to see as other people see. Like sometimes I find it very difficult when somebody doesn't understand where I come from. Or like when I went to America sometimes I was confronted by some people who just couldn't understand that I was a British citizen, they just thought 'Oh, but you look Indian, you cannot be from England'. And it really helped me to understand it better. I mean I'm not saying everything about the course was perfect, but I think I'm always going to take it with me because it's helped me. 'Cos I can see both sides in a way. I can see from a Western point of view, because I've been brought up in England, and I could see it from my culture and my traditions, my family and how we live and how I've been brought up. It's been really helpful to see both points and how there can be otherness and I am the other, but yet I am part of the Western society as well. [Melanie: So what do you think you'll do with that knowledge and understanding?] I don't know. I think I'm just going to, I think it's going to help me throughout my life . . . it's kind of scary in a way as well. . . . what you've learnt but you're scared that if you use it when you're in your business and it's not going to be to your benefit, I don't know, it's just kind of scary, but it's good, it helps me understand, maybe I can make other people understand better when I'm in my own career and stuff.

James: I wouldn't say this course is going to change me as a person. I mean I'm fairly interested in politics, I don't have a vast knowledge of it, but I'm interested in it, you know, and we went over some good political issues and current affairs, talked about current things going on obviously in Afghanistan. The way, you know, [President] Bush feels about it and that and I think it's important in the class to relate to what's going on in the current world. So I got good political knowledge and things from the course but I wouldn't say it's going to change me as a person.

Because capabilities are always multi-dimensional this gaining of critical knowledge and self knowledge also turns on having opportunities for active and participatory learning and for expressive voices – the conditions of respect and recognition that enable speaking. This course required students to grapple with notions of Otherness under conditions of diversity in the class itself, but where the latter conditions were made a strength of the course and enhanced learning. Katrina for example said, 'you have the opportunity to meet people from all over the world, from countries very different from the West'. But Katrina is thoughtful about how she approached this opportunity, commenting later that 'understanding is difficult, there's lots of things I've never seen or even knew they were there and there's lots of things that I do respect but it's difficult to understand because this is something completely different from my own culture'. For those students positioned as the marginalized non-Western Other, the course offered a crucial recognition both of their identities but also offered a critique of Western privilege. A student from Korea found the course empowering in the way it both valued his own culture and brought it into a critical dialogue with white mainstream Western culture in that students were expected to look critically at the privileged place this occupies.

'Mutual respect' (Tasneem) worked in three ways in the class. In the first place, it was valued by students when they debated controversial ideas across a plurality of perspectives, which enabled an expanded understanding. Jasmina put it this way: 'If somebody's coming to you with one argument, you can understand the argument, see your point of view and your position in that argument also'. 'Debate in a class', said James, 'is what you're looking for really, isn't it, debating even with the teacher, I think everybody in the class was interested in it.' Secondly, they worked respectfully with each other, the curriculum was teaching them 'respect for people being different' (James). Thirdly was the lecturer's respect for their ideas so that, said Tasneem, 'If Stephen made a point and someone disagreed with it, if they held their argument and they had facts and backed the argument in a valid way that would be fine for Stephen. He did not say, "Oh no this is my point of view" '.

As Sennett (2003: 226) reminds us, mutual respect is not just some 'tool to grease the gears of society' but such exchanges 'turn people outward – a stance which is necessary for the development of character'.

In this group of students, then, I interpret the capabilities that were valued by some or all members of the focus group as these: (i) critical knowledge generating critical thought; (ii) respecting, recognizing, valuing diversity and difference; (iii) reflective self knowledge; (iv) participatory and active learning and having a voice which is heard and listened to; and (v) being able to engage a plurality of views in dialogue and debate.

3. Professional education, an example from town planning

In my third example groups of final year town planning students reflect on a fourth year module on 'Protection of the Environment'. Here I am most concerned with two focus group student interviews with six students on 19 April 2002 and another six on 28 March 2003. (Data included two interviews with the lecturer and a number of informal conversations, interviews with volunteer focus groups over two years, course materials, and a whole-class questionnaire in 2002.)

Briefly turning first to the lecturer (interview 21 March 2002), he is concerned that as a profession, town planners fail 'to strongly engage with the deepest value conflicts that surround their work' to which there are seldom 'easy' solutions. Instead, he hopes that students learn that the planning process is 'inherently political', saturated with value conflicts, and that they grapple with the kinds of practices that need to flow from this awareness. The point is that students learn both technical skills and a critical understanding of the planning process. The struggle is then to translate these ideas into pedagogical action, which this lecturer has attempted through experimenting with different approaches and through talking to colleagues with similar concerns and commitments to teaching. Early on, resistant feedback on a lecture course in which he and a colleague tried to 'push at the students, to challenge them' about serious environmental issues 'in quite a forceful way', 'just taking the whole thing head on and almost pushing a message at the students' encountered instead a 'wall of defence' – 'they just tried to ignore some of the stuff we were putting across to them'. This teaching approach would be characterized by Arendt (1977) as crushing newness by 'striking from students' hands' the opportunity to think anew. The capability to be talked at was not valued by students.

This experience led the lecturer to develop more interactive and dialogical problem-based approaches in which a plurality of perspectives is generated through the pedagogy of the course. Students take up 'stakeholder' positions, which are often not their own, towards environmental issues and use a dialogical process to understand diverse and conflicting points of view. The discussion-based sessions take on the different forms which students might encounter in actual professional situations – for example a public meeting, or a closed-door round table conference – and in which the rules for engagement work differently in each case. They must struggle with other stakeholders to get their own views heard and to persuade others. Because the students themselves hold different views on what constitutes the best approach to particular environmental issues, they have to work hard at listening to each other in order to construct knowledge about town planning. For example, students work in small groups with a variety of resource materials and then have to take up and defend diverse stakeholder positions in relation to renewable energy policy such as wind farms. Stakeholders might include the national park authority, the renewable energy industry, a local countryside pressure group, government, and so on. At issue is that such dilemmas do not lend themselves to a straightforward resolution. Confronted with different stakeholder views, students have to grapple with solutions which might lead industry to desert a rural area, with severe economic consequences, or contribute to rural environmental blight by erecting a wind farm.

Faced with such apparently intractable dilemmas, students are not abandoned to hopeless uncertainty. Instead the course attempts to enable them to learn how to deliberate in contexts of value conflict so that they might develop greater insights into the complexity of the problems. At the same time Arendt's natality – the new, the unpredictable, the unexpected – is enabled. The lecturer has a position on these dilemmas but works to 'leave it open for the students to look at it how they want . . . there's a lot of room for interpretation and debate, it's not hard and fast, I'm quite open about where it goes' (interview, 21 March 2002). Students have to learn how to deliberate across differences both in their small groups, and in the plenary group.

The 2002 students, reflecting on the process of learning to deliberate across diverse and conflicting points of view, explained, for example, that:

> One of the good things of working in groups is that the two people I worked with came from different viewpoints to me. . . . Quite often there are conflicts between different people's points of view and perhaps you can't reconcile the conflicts but you can manage them and by trying to get local communities involved with the planning process you can better work out what different people's viewpoints are and then from there try to mitigate and compensate some of the things that people will lose through the planning process by having to make concessions to other parties and create balance in the process . . . it's quite easy just to look at policy and not consider communities . . . I suppose this project taught us to think about the communities we're going to be serving . . . people have to live with your decisions . . . you have to be aware of the different power relationships and resources among the people you're going to be working with.
>
> (Kevin)

David explained further that he had learned that the dominant planning model of dictating to communities was flawed and that he now understood why planning ought to engage affected communities and 'try to make the whole process more transparent for them, and accountable so they can see the decisions going on'. An ethical awareness of power relationships, they had learnt, was crucial – who had the money and the expertise – and with this the need to 'positively discriminate' (Debra) in the interests of those with less power. They had become 'more empathic' (Christine) to different people who take part in the planning process.

Exposure to a plurality of perspectives 'makes you realise that just coming in with the same opinion and looking at things in the same way every time stifles innovation and it stops you from being as good at planning as you could be if you were willing to have a more open mind' (Mark). Students commented that they had realized how their own value judgements make it difficult for them to understand the perspective of others with different perspectives and interests, because 'we already have a reaction lined up in our minds'. What they had to learn through deliberation was a considered empathy by defending positions which they found unsympathetic to their own points of view, and the value of 'rough and ready' compromises rather than situations 'where nobody backed down'. Tom explained that theory 'has to be grounded in real life examples, like how would it affect the old woman who lives in the cottage in the conservation area'. They further valued the process of active learning which required them to undertake research, and publicly develop and defend a 'really solid argument' (David) to their peers, and develop confidence in the 'safe' environment of the classroom. The students found that this process of having to manage conflict in arriving at decisions, and of having to put aside their own positions to take on that of stakeholders generated more creative problem-solving and know-ledge construction. At the same time, they were acquiring critical knowledge and learning that 'you don't have to accept everything you receive. . . . and it opened things up for me because throughout school you're taught "these are the facts" ' (Tom).

The group welcomed the space for independent, active and experiential learning, doing their own research from books and on the Internet, forming an argument and then having to publicly present and defend it. This was better, Mark said, 'than just sitting at the back of the classroom and having someone lecturing at you . . . it doesn't bring the issues to life'. He explained that seeing words on the board and even writing them down does not neces-sarily encourage you to think about the issue, whereas 'if people are asking you awkward questions you're forced to think about the issues'.

The second focus group evaluated this module in 2003, commenting on how they too valued being exposed to a practical process of 'managing con-flict' in urban planning decision making in which they had to 'just sort out what was the better argument' (Kate). They valued the way the pedagogical process had enabled their access to abstract concepts about consensus build-ing by having them engage in experiential learning. Molly summed up when she said, 'I've learnt an awful lot from the course. . . . about democratic processes. . . . and it's just got me thinking about a whole load of things'. It was 'incredibly interesting' (Tim), having 'to leave your own positions at the door and just sort out what was the better argument . . . the best thing to aim for is to try and put yourself in other people's shoes and to look at it from that perspective' (Kate). 'I think it's got to be a better option for planning because often you're dealing with complex issues which involve lots of people', explained Hannah, while Lily affirmed that, 'It's terribly important to be open-minded whatever you do'. The knowledge and the knowing gained on the course were seen as crucial for 'enabling' practice (Joe); or for trying to alter a system which tends to override the interests of people, 'for example the way waste incinerators and landfill sites just get dumped on the doorsteps of people who already have multiple deprivation' (Kate).

Students had become aware of how power works in discussion forums. They said they had developed an awareness and respect for the process of decision making, rather than just focusing on outcomes, and a reflective awareness of professional action. Sarah explained that:

> I used to think the ends justified the means. I used to think the outcome was all important and now, since I started doing this course, I firmly believe that it's the process that's important. I'm going to be a different planner now than the one I think I would have been . . . I wouldn't have thought it was necessarily a bad thing to go into planning meetings and actually impose what I thought was best and now I think that was probably not a good thing.

Tim, on the other hand, had come to the view that there was some kind of middle way between imposition and deliberation in real world contexts where planners needed to be able to recognize where to apply leverage, in his case, in order to promote the interests of the 'urban poor'. His professional aspiration was to be 'an enabler' of the voices of people who might not otherwise get heard.

Over time, students came to value the way their lecturer, having set the pedagogical scene, would not impose his own point of view. Conditioned by educational experiences to the security of the teacher having the right answer or the last word, students wanted this at the start of the module, gradually shifting in the face of the teacher 'letting learn'. Thus Hannah commented that at first, the lecturer not giving them an answer at the end of the sessions, 'felt a bit like not that we'd failed but like we couldn't reach a decision. . . . but then I realised that wasn't really what it was about, it was about the process and learning about the process . . . he didn't say "I don't feel that was the right conclusion" or "I thought you were going in the wrong direction" '.

The students in both groups also valued the social relations of learning, small things like being able to exchange telephone numbers and so discuss any problems on the course, and knowing others on the course so that 'if we recognised somebody walking around the university or working in the library we could always start a conversation with them' (Stephen). Paradoxically, Stephen said, these friendships made it easier to conduct respectful but challenging class dialogues because people knew 'we weren't doing it just to wind each other up'. In the 2002 group, David explained that you had to come up with a really good argument 'so that you get your mates to shut up'. 'You can't blag', said Kevin, 'you've got to really think about the issues'. On the other hand, the classroom provided a space to practise arguments and develop confidence 'in a fairly safe environment' (Debra). Moreover there was a productive sharing of work and knowledge because people in the class knew what their colleagues had worked on. Someone working on a particular topic for their fourth year dissertation might borrow a relevant essay from someone else, 'rather than people going off secretly doing a random essay title and handing it in with no-one knowing' (David). Their work and their learning thus became more transparent to each other.

In this case, I suggest that the capabilities that these students valued were: (i) being able to relate theory to practice; (ii) social relations of learning; (iii) developing understanding from a plurality of perspectives; (iv) knowledge of the process of deliberative democracy and inequalities of power; (v) acquiring the professional knowledge to support the excluded and marginalized in planning decision making; (vi) active, reflective and experiential learning; and, (vii) knowledge for professional action in the world.

Higher education capabilities

In discussion, then, all these students identified what processes enabled them to acquire and demonstrate, both in talk and writing for assessment, what we might call higher-order thinking, critical knowledge and deep understanding. Their voices point to conditions of support for and confidence in learning, of provocation to thinking, of independence in thinking, and of respect and recognition of differences in perspectives and identities. We might describe this in capability terms as the development of reasoning, or rationality. The particular pedagogical contexts enable their educational opportunity, or we might say freedom, to develop such rationality for present and future choices and valued identities. Students identify what they found valuable and what they gained from the courses they had studied, not only for their present lives in higher education, but also their futures beyond as lawyers, teachers, researchers, managers, town planners, and so on. I call these capabilities – valuable beings. They are multi-dimensional, pointing to positive changes in students' understanding of the subject, of their own agency achievement, and of future possibilities 'in shaping their own destiny' (Sen, 1999: 53).

I emphasize again that no claim is made that these student voices are representative of anything other than these particular course experiences. Instead what is demonstrated here is a method of student participation and reflection in identifying valuable capabilities which might then contribute to producing a provisional list. It is to this that I turn in Chapter 6, taking into account the 'capability narratives' presented in this and the next chapter.

Notes

1 The data for these examples was originally collected as part of a research and development project 'Teaching For Critical Learning' in 2002–2003, which took the form of evaluating selected courses at three universities in which lecturers were concerned to develop through their teaching a form of Barnett's (1997) criticality. Data was collected through in-depth interviews with volunteer students, the lecturers involved, and the scrutiny of relevant course documents. In all cases students, lecturers and their universities have been anonymized. Other courses in Law, Information Studies, Sociology and French were also considered but are not drawn on here. Two of the three universities are part of the élite 18 'Russell Group' of British universities, and the third a 1960s' 'Robbins' university. Generally all these universities are better funded and most will have stronger research performance profiles than the newer, post-1992 universities, which were previously either polytechnics or colleges of higher education. Teaching loads are heavier than they have been in the past but better than in less well-resourced universities, and competition for student places on most courses is likely to be strong. These contextual conditions will have a shaping effect, but arguably as strong an effect lies in the disciplinary discourse and the teacher's assumptions about student learning and his or her commitments to teaching.

5
Widening Participation and Capabilities

There is too often a failure to imagine how social class is actually lived on the pulse, how it informs our inner worlds as it conditions our chances in the outer world.

(Annette Kuhn, *Family Secrets*, 1995: 1001)

This chapter continues with my project, begun in the previous chapter, to explore pedagogy through the lens of the capability approach, and draws in particular on Nussbaum's (2000a) work, in a kind of 'conversation' with another group of student voices. It further illustrates a method of student voice in selecting valued capabilities. My focus here is on 'widening partici-pation' in England, that is enabling working class students, currently only 20% of the cohort who enter higher education (Archer *et al.*, 2003), to participate and succeed as learners. What emerges from the work of Watts and Bridges (2003), and also that of Reay (2004) and Brine and Waller (2004) is the significance of the capability of risk-taking for working class students – risk in choosing higher education, risk in choosing particular universities, and risk in negotiating and navigating their way through. The talk of Reay's mature students is resonant with notions of comfort, safety and belonging versus the risk of failure and the shame of 'being made to feel I wasn't up to it' (quoted in Reay, 2004: 36). Similarly, Sasha in Brine and Waller (2004: 105) struggles with the risk of her own academic failure, say-ing, 'It took quite a lot of guts to pluck up the courage and try it [university access course], to risk it. Failure could have such a bad effect on me . . . In a way it would have been easier not to do it'. It may therefore be that this capability of risk needs to be incorporated into a provisional list as a valuable capability. I return to this later.

To reiterate, pedagogy as noted in Chapter 1, means teaching methods in the widest sense. It is not a neutral relay for knowledge but value-laden, biography-saturated and takes place under specific institutional and policy conditions of possibility. It contains the potentiality of both normalization and equity, of reproduction and change (see also Chapter 6). Core to my

concerns in this chapter continues to be that experiences in higher education build over time into inter-subjective patterns and shape what kind of
persons we recognize ourselves to be and what we believe ourselves able to
do. Answers to practical educational questions about what knowledge to
teach, using what pedagogy, and to whom, express judgements about which
aspects of existing forms of social life ought to be reproduced and to be
transformed if all learners are to be prepared for the world of the future.
Conversely, questions about how society ought to be improved and changed
also take form as educational questions about the kind of knowledge,
attitudes and skills that participation in improved forms of social life requires.

The chapter now proceeds from education policy developed in England,
which outlines important inclusion goals:

> Education must be a force for opportunity and social justice, not for the
> entrenchment of privilege. We must make certain that the opportunities
> that higher education brings are available to all those who have the
> potential to benefit from them, regardless of their background. This is
> not just about preventing active discrimination; it is about working
> actively to make sure that potential is recognised and fostered wherever
> it is found.
>
> (Department for Education and Science, 2003: 67)

At issue then is how we evaluate how well we are doing in working towards
such goals. How do we evaluate equality achievements in relation to widening participation? For example, here is an apparently successful educational
outcome. Two young women both complete a degree in English literature at
the same English university. For one, from a middle class, reasonably affluent
background and a good school, a major reason was her decision to experience university before entering her father's business as a trainee manager.
Thus an outstanding degree result was not required, although she coped
well with the academic demands having been suitably prepared by her
schooling and the advice of her graduate parents. She chose rather to spend
her time socializing and pursuing her leisure interests of cycling and music.
The second young woman, from a working class background and a not very
good state school, worked long hours in poorly paid part-time jobs to supplement her student loan, had very little spare money to socialize, lived in
cheap accommodation and ate cheap food. Despite significant academic
ability, she struggled to fit in and her lack of confidence meant she was
reluctant to approach her tutors for help with work, for which her school
had not prepared her well. Both students obtain second class passes. Can we
then say that the inclusion goal has been met for the working class student,
who apparently did as well as her middle class counterpart? Can we say that
this example demonstrates equality; and if so, 'equality of what'? My argument is that the capabilities approach enables us to address the real
opportunities that influence the achievements of both these students, that it
reveals that there is no genuine equality of achievement or agency, and that
pedagogy is a significant component of a student's opportunity set.

Capabilities and equality pedagogy

How then might capabilities take us forward in dealing positively with diversity? Nussbaum argues for a life that is 'truly human'; such a life is characterized by freedom, autonomy and an active agency exercised in co-operation and reciprocity with others. Her list of 10 central human capabilities[1] is incommensurable and multi-dimensional. They have, she says, 'broad cross-cultural resonance and intuitive power' (2000a: 72). If Nussbaum's capabilities were to inform higher education pedagogy and curricula, they would, I believe, require inclusive higher education processes and cultures: access, knowledge, ways of knowing, participation and progression by diverse students.

Nussbaum points to 'practical reason' and 'affiliation' in her list of 10 central capabilities, as being of special importance; they are architectonic. Practical reason she describes as, 'Being able to form a conception of the good and to engage in critical reflection about planning one's life' (2000a: 79). Affiliation involves social relations, respect and equal valuing of difference. She describes this capability as:

> Being able to live with and toward others, to recognize and show concern for other human beings, to engage in various forms of social interaction; to be able to imagine the situation of another and to have compassion for that situation; to have the capability for both justice and friendship. . . . having the social bases of self–respect and non-humiliation; being able to be treated as a dignified being whose worth is equal to that of others. This entails at a minimum protections against discrimination on the basis of race, sex, sexual orientation, religion, caste, ethnicity, or national origin. In work being able to work as a human being, exercising practical reason and entering into meaningful relationships of mutual recognition with other workers.
>
> (2000a: 79–80)

She explains further that:

> Among the capabilities, two, practical reason and affiliation, stand out as of special importance, since they both organise and suffuse all the others, making their pursuit truly human. To use one's senses in a way not infused by the characteristically human use of thought and planning is to use them in an incompletely human manner. To plan for one's own life without being able to do so in complex forms of discourse, concern and reciprocity with other human beings is, again, to behave in an incompletely human way. To take just one example, work, to be a truly human mode of functioning, must involve the availability of both practical reason and affiliation. It must involve being able to behave as a thinking being, not just a cog in a machine, and it must be capable of being done with and towards others in a way that involves mutual recognition of humanity.
>
> (2000a: 82)

For 'work' we could substitute study in higher education. We might also argue that practical reason develops our capability to own and take responsibility for our own lives and the consequences for and on others; while affiliation means developing our capability for showing consideration to others, for understanding them, for participating ethically in the human condition.

These two capabilities alone would be a demanding basis for evaluating learning, agency and well-being in and through higher education pedagogy.

The capability of practical reason

Higher education for the 14 students in my Widening Participation Project[2] was for the most part a place where they had the opportunity (freedom) to plan their lives, to consider their hopes and aspirations for a better life, and to develop their own views of what for them would be a good life. For all the troubles they might have encountered during their studies – and evidence was uneven across the 14 individuals – they were all clear that higher education had expanded their life choices. Here are illustrative examples of practical reasoning from these students. First, Katie talks about the future she does not want and can now escape:

> This is what I want to avoid, being stuck in a shop for the rest of my life, being unhappy in my job, just dreading going to work . . . my mum hates her job and the thing she says to me is 'If I tell you one thing, don't do a job that you hate, do something that you want to do'. . . . It's [university] making it clearer what I actually want to do with my life, because I don't know, actually learning the law, yeah I want to do this, this is really interesting. I do want to find out more about this . . . Basically it's just giving me confidence. I know who I am and I'm just happier at university. . . . There are lots of people who if I wasn't at university I would never have met. It has extended the people that I wouldn't necessarily have spoken to and got to know.
>
> (interview, 10 May 2002)

Matt who had switched from engineering to biology said:

> I've become much more independent. I would say I've matured since I've come to university. I've met new people, done new things, I've been in control of my life a bit more . . . It sort of prepares you for life and it's a sort of halfway house between still living at home and having the backing of your parents but at the same time also not living at home and you're doing things your own way. . . . If I hadn't come to university . . . I would still have been living at home and I think my mum and dad would have tried to exercise a lot more control over me, whereas by coming to university I've got total freedom.
>
> (interview, 14 May 2002)

Towards the end of her degree studies, Narinder said that her choices had become 'more open-ended' and 'you start to think about all the things you can do', whereas before she thought she had stayed within 'safe' boundaries of home and neighbourhood, but university has 'sort of pushed my potential' (interview, 20 May 2003). Rosie commented that, 'I realise now how much I was an extension really of my mum and my sister and now I just feel completely separate from them and different . . . so I think I've got the independence and the freedom and the confidence to do different things' (interview, 20 May 2003). Janet explained her hopes for the future:

> I hope by coming to university I've to some extent secured the fact that I'll get a job, I'll get a career. I hope I'm going to be fairly financially secure with whatever job I'm in because . . . I hope to have people I'm close to as well. I don't want to pursue a career and be so into that it's at the cost of family or friendships, 'cos I think you'd end up isolated and feeling alone.
>
> (interview, 10 May 2003)

Of course, what Nussbaum has in mind in outlining her approach is capability – not functioning – although she does also acknowledge that where capabilities are of particular importance we may well need also to pay attention to functioning (see Chapter 3). In the examples above, we see students exercising their capability of practical reason, that is their functioning, and in this way we might claim that they are developing this key capability. Nonetheless, what they choose to do with their lives after university cannot be pre-determined. As Arendt explains: 'The problem is simply to educate in such a way that a setting-right [of the world] remains actually possible, even though it can, of course, never be assured' (1977: 192).

The capability of affiliation

Affiliation is for Nussbaum another architectonic capability. With its emphasis on social relations it is arguably central to pedagogical interactions, to relationships between lecturers and students and between students and students that support learning and positive learner identities (Blake *et al.*, 1998; Thomas 2002; Reay, 2004). Thomas (2002) cites working class students who say that tutors who care about students learning foster their self-confidence and the disposition to learn and make an effort. But affiliation can also be diminished in higher education for working class students. Thus Narinder wrote in her diary that: 'It is so impersonal at university, it's like the lecturers don't care. I find this slightly intimidating. If I had a problem I really would think twice before approaching someone, everyone seems so busy and at a distance, asking for help comes across as being a failure'. This affects her sense of agency so that she has to remind herself, 'I know I'm intelligent . . . but it doesn't seem enough, maybe it is just me but everyone seems a lot cleverer than me. My friend who does the same course asked her academic tutor for help and he made her feel rubbish. She is someone that's been doing consistently well but somehow has lost the ability to do well' (diary entry, 28 May 2002).

This is exacerbated in that working class students often expect to do less well or to be less confident than their peers, as Narinder suggests. In the worst cases this failure to flourish may lead to students dropping out altogether.

Affiliation also plays itself out in the lives of widening participation students in the friendships and social networks they forge at university. Nussbaum (1990: 44) reminds us of the importance of friendship in our becoming 'good perceivers' [learners], that is, able to read a situation and single out what is relevant for thought and action. We need to trust in the guidance offered and allow ourselves to feel engaged with a friend's life and choices, to share a form of life with them. This further highlights the deep problem if students are alienated from each other because they do not feel comfortable in higher education. Diane Reay (2004: 35) cites a mature working class student, Janice, who says, 'I don't see the point of spending my time with people who are not going to be able to relate to me and I'm not going to be able to relate to them'. Friendships were crucial in supporting students in the Widening Participation Project. They placed great emphasis on their friendships at university, not least as they loosened their ties with friends at home. 'I've not kept in touch with them' is a common refrain. This is similar to the findings of Thomas (2002) and Forbes and Wickens (2005) who argue that friendship is one of the keys to persistence and success among working class students. One might argue that friendship is both an 'opportunity capability' – the freedom to pursue our gaols, and a 'process capability' – the freedom involved in the process of this pursuit, was the person obstructed or helped, and so on (see Sen, 2002: 9–13).

Its significance in relation to pedagogy in particular is in generating a feeling of belonging on your course and being able to get along with your peers, so that Rosie says of her middle class peers, 'I wouldn't say I'd like to socialise with them and talk about, you know, personal things, but when we're talking about work or we're doing work, then it's fine. I don't mind, friendly in that way, like as a colleague kind of a way' (interview 7 May 2002). Janet said she had liked working in a smaller group for a seminar: 'We all know each other and we'd talked before and stuff so we'd just get on with it and then we did the presentation. It was easier that we all knew each other' (interview 18 May 2002). This is not to say that this kind of collaborative work is unproblematic; it can be frustrating, it can diminish capability if a student feels excluded in her classes. Janet also made sure to develop friendships with 'like-minded' people where work is concerned, saying that 'I'm never going to get anything done if you're sitting with those people who aren't doing anything'.

Friends also offer someone to turn to, to discuss difficulties with the work, and often working class students will prefer this to approaching their tutors. For example, Norah recounted that when she does not know what is going on in her literature class, she feels stupid, and remains silent. But she then tries to sort things out for herself by asking a close friend what she makes of the work, or seeing if she can find help on the Internet. But she says, 'I'd rarely go and see a tutor if I had a problem' (interview, 29 May 2002). This is arguably more important to working class students whose parents are not familiar with higher education and restricted thus in what advice they are able to offer in decoding how higher education works, beyond generally encouraging their children to study and supporting them in their decisions. In other words, it is arguably harder for working class students to seek help and build networks with 'institutional agents' who have 'the capacity and commitment to transmit directly, or negotiate the transmission of, institutional resources and opportunities' (Stanton-Salazar, 1997: 6). Where students do develop a good relationship with a tutor or lecturer this supports their learning in important ways. Narinder, for example, described her personal tutor as someone she could always go and talk to, someone who helped her with her academic work, someone she could really relate to (interview, 28 May 2002).

On the other hand, approaching tutors for help can have less satisfactory outcomes. When Janet e-mailed a lecturer for advice about the mismatch between a marker's comments on an essay she had written and the actual essay, the response was unhelpful, 'she just sort of sent it back saying "Well, I haven't seen the work, I didn't mark the essay, I can't really comment", and said that perhaps it's more my problem and that I'm finding it difficult to adjust to university work'. Although Janet felt she was coping as well as others on her course, because the lecturer seemed to think she was 'struggling' with the work Janet in turn began to feel that maybe she was not fitting in as well as she had thought, or coping as well as she thought (interview, 18 May, 2002). What is interesting here is how learner identities are formed and their capabilities fostered or diminished in these everyday small instances of interaction, which if not interrupted build into patterns, over time, of diminished academic confidence. Students also compare themselves to others on their courses, and for those from non-traditional backgrounds this can be harder on their confidence. For example, Matt found out quite quickly that he had chosen the wrong degree programme but he said:

> I just buried my head in the sand and thought eventually it would work out. I didn't go and see the lecturers, not one of them. I think it was, I didn't want to seem as though I was struggling because everybody else was finding it easy and I thought well surely if they're finding it easy, I should find it easy and the longer I left it the harder it became . . . I left it and left it and left it'.
>
> (interview, 14 May 2002)

When he did finally pluck up courage to go and talk to one of the lecturers 'he made me feel really small and insignificant'.

The wider importance which cannot entirely be disentangled from the self students bring to their pedagogical encounters is the effect through living and social arrangements on confidence and belonging. Most students if not living at home will live in residential halls in their first year and meet the students with whom they will also be studying, making the transition into classes somewhat easier. Those living at home and with less opportunity to meet new friends in halls of residence or flats, worry especially about how they will fit in. Thus Janet gets on with those in her class but feels closest to Kay, a mature student from a working class background. Friendships generate important emotional resources during a time of significant and often 'scary' personal changes of surviving and coping – living away from home, meeting people many of whom are from different backgrounds and few from similar class backgrounds, managing money, finding part-time work, and encountering new and challenging learning experiences.

Friendships also provide what Wedekind (2001: 198) calls 'identity capital', which he defines as 'information one acquires that tells one that one is wanted, loved, or recognised as being a member of a group', and new forms of social capital and norms of reciprocity in these new communities of practice. Rosie's working class friends at university seemed central to her shoring up her working class identity; all her housemates shared similar class backgrounds. Again, the impact of these social experiences on the context of students' learning can also be negative. Jackie did not live in halls in her first year, and described her experience in the history course of 'feeling isolated . . . everybody completely ignored me' because they already knew each other from the halls of residence. She continued, 'they made no attempt to speak to anyone who wasn't from their hall . . . it was horrible and I was so depressed by the end of that week . . . I had about five hours of lectures a week and apart from lectures I just spent all the time in my room on my own'. On the other hand she found students on her English course 'very different' and here she felt 'really at home, I like the students, the tutors are lovely' (interview, 15 May 2002).

Thomas (2002) argues that institutions can facilitate the development of social networks and that this illustrates the close interrelationship between the academic and social experiences of working class students. Higher education is far from being an egalitarian or a democratic space. We need to consider changing both our public institutions and the lives of individuals (while women comprise a majority of undergraduate students in higher education in the UK, for example, universities continue as resolutely masculinist institutions). Nussbaum (2002) argues for institutional responsibilities in promoting human capabilities. We need therefore to take up practically Sen's (1999) emphasis on integrating intrapersonal and interpersonal freedoms (individual agency and social arrangements). We should not, he and Dreze (1995) argue, view individuals and their opportunities in isolated terms. Crucially, functionings depend on individual circumstances, the relations a person has with others, and social conditions and contexts within which potential options (freedom) can be achieved. Francis Stewart (2004) has argued that we need also to go beyond the capability approach emphasis on the individual (albeit socially located) and consider what she describes as 'group capabilities'. She argues that groups and group membership are a direct source of well-being. While she is arguing for the importance of groups for the poor, we might argue that groups are crucial to working class and other non-traditional students in higher education and that we need to consider how groups promote values and preferences which then foster valuable capabilities. Janet's joining groups of like-minded hardworking students both at school and in university might be one such example. Whether one can convincingly argue that group capabilities are anything more than the sum of their individual capabilities could be contested. Nonetheless, from a policy point of view the importance of those institutional factors which foster co-operation and communication within and between diverse groups is at issue. Such group formation and affiliation is a source of power, and Stewart (2004) argues that we should support groups which encourage valuable capabilities as against those which do the opposite. Such groups would, she says, also teach tolerance of multiple cultural identities co-existing. This further underlines the social nature of learning and the argument made by Thomas (2002) and borne out in my own work of the importance of inclusive approaches which respect and value differences amongst students, and institutional measures to support such approaches. At issue here is that the capability of affiliation as outlined by Nussbaum, and as it emerges in its importance for working class students, is a demanding criterion for evaluating pedagogical practices.

The capability of emotions

To the capabilities of practical reason and affiliation as valuable for working class students' educational flourishing, we might now also add Nussbaum's capability of 'emotions'. She describes this as:

> Being able to have attachments to things and people outside ourselves; to love those who love and care for us, to grieve at their absence; in general to love, to grieve, to experience longing, gratitude, and justified anger. Not having one's emotional development blighted by over-whelming fear or anxiety.

> (2000a: 79)

Rosie's comment here is saturated with emotion as she says, pointing to a photograph she has taken of the University of Sheffield's library building: 'You just see the library from the outside and it just seems so important, it looks so big and scary; if I hadn't been to university, I would always have felt kind of jealous and thought "I wonder what they're learning in there?" ' (interview, 17 May 2002).

Nussbaum (2001: 19) argues that emotions 'involve judgements about important things'; they shape our mental lives and are a source of knowledge and understanding. Discernment is central to wise practice, and discernment is mobilized through imagination and emotions (Dunne and Pendlebury, 2003). Fear is a barrier to learning and to confidence in our ability to learn. When we feel resentful, upset, frightened, hostile, nervous, humiliated, alienated, we do not learn well. These kinds of emotions are a kind of social control which uphold existing relations of power and intellectual valuing in higher education pedagogies (Boler, 1999). Nussbaum emphasizes that supporting the capability of emotions involves supporting the associational forms that are crucial to this capability. This, I argue, includes pedagogical forms in higher education. Thus, one working class student from the Widening Participation Project wrote in his diary about his experiences of history seminars at university: 'I used to really, REALLY hate doing seminars. I would get very nervous, my hands would sweat and my voice would shake'. He has developed some confidence in presenting a topic to the rest of the group but when it is over feels that 'at least I now have nothing else to worry about for a month or so'. If others feel like him, it is not surprising that there is limited participation in the group, nor does the tutor seem to know how to encourage this. Thus, he writes, 'What usually occurs is that someone will read out their presentation, silence will follow and then, after much prompting a few people will talk about what they know until the lecturer gets desperate and delivers what amounts to an informal lecture. . . . After a week of late nights and early mornings no-one really had the energy to feign much interest and the seminar finished early' (Tom, diary entry, 9 April 2002). Jackie, who continued to struggle through her first year, described battling with a course on literary theory, saying, 'I thought I really don't understand this and I got myself in such a state it made me feel really depressed all term . . . there was no reason to be here anymore' (interview, 15 May 2002). This is not to eschew dissonance and confusion, which is part of the challenge of higher learning. Rather it is to say that some students will need support in recognizing this confusion as part of learning, and not as a sign of failing.

When we feel excited, involved, engaged, confident we are more likely to want to participate in learning, to be keenly responsive, and to learn well. Thus Widening Participation students in my study also spoke about the rich pleasures of intellectual work. Jackie commented that, 'It was like something clicked inside, something suddenly got switched on . . . and suddenly I could write these essays, and I was actually enjoying writing them'. She discussed an oral presentation which the tutor had described as 'very well researched'. 'That kept me smiling all day', she said (interview, 15 May 2002). Norah explained that 'I just get a buzz out of it. I actually get a thrill out of sitting there and working something out, like if you get a really good idea especially with English because there's like no answers, it's all sort of what you interpret and if you have a strong idea you apply it . . . I really do enjoy seminars a lot'. Even though she procrastinates in getting reading and written work done, 'when I actually start doing it I think, my god this is what I love doing, why haven't I been doing it' (interview, 29 May 2002). Rosie talked about completing an essay on Shakespeare where she had really enjoyed going to the library and 'churning through the critics' and reading the Shakespeare, 'taking it to pieces and seeing the professor and seeing what he said about it and writing it and having to think really really hard, what do I actually believe and having to order my ideas. I really enjoyed writing it. I got a first for it as well' (interview, 17 May 2002). In these pedagogical moments new possibilities arise, a love of knowledge is developed, and capability is enhanced.

We have then three related 'educational capabilities', none of which can be reduced to one of the others, from Nussbaum's list: (i) practical reason, (ii) affiliation and (iii) emotions, all of which are arguably especially important in widening participation pedagogies. That not all of the 10 capabilities on Nussbaum's list are key capabilities in the space of education should not be a problem, notwithstanding Nussbaum's argument that all the capabilities on her list are of central importance, and none can be left out. Nussbaum after all details a list that includes but goes beyond education to provide the basis for a decent social (not just educational) minimum. Pedagogically, the capabilities of practical reason and affiliation in particular are a more subtle and complex working out of teaching methods of 'group' or 'teamwork' to include values of empathy and mutual recognition, compassion, respect, dignity, active voices, and meaningful relationships with peers. Nussbaum's capabilities approach, if taken up pedagogically, should enable both critical knowledge making and collective problem solving through processes of critical dialogue, respect, inclusion of diverse perspectives and 'reasonableness', that is, the willingness to listen to others whose views, histories and experiences differ from one's own. Practising affiliation as part of higher education pedagogy would tend towards deliberation which opens out a transformative space in which, through democratic dialogue with others different from oneself, we gain new ideas which enable our critical reflection on our own positions, prejudices or ignorance as women and men, working class and middle class, black and white. At issue here also is that at school or university we do not just learn mathematics, or philosophy or history; we also learn ways of being, whether to be open minded or fair or generous spirited, or none of these things. We might learn in higher education how to do gender or race or social class differently. Thus middle class students need to learn how their own privilege works, as much as working class students need equal valuing and support to acquire the cultural and social capital of the university *on their own terms*.

Risk, opportunity and preferences

My concern is specifically with how pedagogy shapes student identities (valuable beings and doings and choices) in ways which inflect towards or away from equality of capabilities. I have argued in the previous chapters that this is for me a convincing way to evaluate educational development and social justice in higher education. How pedagogy works was mentioned in previous chapters refracted through the voices of Paula Rothenberg, Beverley Skeggs, Louise Morley, bell hooks, and others less well known like Sara Covington. Here are further examples of experiences of pedagogy at work in normalizing existing power and class relations. In the first, a student who is the first in her family to attend university explained in an interview that students from 'good' schools seemed much more confident than her, more 'expansive' as she put it, so that in university classes, 'they seemed to be able to sort of argue and discuss things and I felt like a little thing in the corner ... I never knew anyone who had been to university, I didn't know what to expect when I got there ... I'd never been in that sort of situation or even seen it before or heard any stories about it or anything' (quoted in Walker, 2001b: 7). In my second example, Janet, a young woman from the Widening Participation Project explained to me that:

> We had a Sociology seminar and we were talking about our backgrounds and how we got to university. And some of the people were saying, I think a couple had parents who didn't go to university but they still said they were more middle class and they don't identify with the working class. It was just as if people don't really want to say they're working class ... I don't know if they feel ashamed of it but I just said I think I'm working class 'cos I grew up in a working class area and have working class parents ... I just say that I am [working class] but when other people are saying 'Oh I don't think I'm working class', as if there's something really negative about that, as if you're like someone different or something, so it makes you feel a bit uneasy at times.
>
> (quoted in Walker, 2006: forthcoming).

My third example is from a black working class woman in London in Archer *et al.*'s (2003) study. They quoted her as saying: 'I'm just coming from an [university] access course, it's about I mean, more higher level. It's like I'm just trying to look in, learning how to break down – but some of the terms, I don't know ... Because when he's giving the lecture and he's like talking, talking, talking, saying those words and things. I said, my God, I don't know what you're saying! I'm lost.' (quoted in Archer *et al.*, 2003: 133). Finally, explaining how social structures and arrangements shape what goes on in universities more broadly, bell hooks (1994: 177) writes, 'From grade school on, we are all encouraged to cross the threshold of the classroom believing we are entering a democratic space – a free zone where the desire to study and learn makes us all equal'. Instead she found pedagogical processes during her college years in the USA valued only middle class norms and demeanour. To avoid estrangement (or what Mann might describe as alienation, see Chapter 1), students from working-class backgrounds like herself, she found, had to assimilate into the mainstream ways of talking and being.

Because pedagogy is a carrier for relations of power and privilege, what we need, Barr (2002: 322) argues, is a system of higher education 'which is not an apprenticeship into a hierarchy of power', operating exclusions against what counts as knowledge and who may be counted as knowers. In particular therefore I draw on Nussbaum (2000a) in this chapter and seek to apply her approach to capability from the perspective of social class in higher education. Her capability approach and her specific list of 10 capabilities (2000a: 78–81, and see Chapter 6) has been explored for its contribution to a conceptualization and practice of justice in higher education, and as one answer to the question 'how well are we doing in supporting widening participation students to succeed in higher education?'

As noted in earlier chapters, the capability approach highlights the limitations of evaluating human development in terms of individual preference satisfaction, or utility measures. We adapt our preferences and our desires, according to what we think is possible for us. Thus Nussbaum (2000a: 114) writes of how 'habit, fear, low expectations and unjust background conditions deform people's choices and even wishes for their own lives'. 'The desire for a college [university] education', she declares, 'is not a brute fact of Nature but is shaped by what you think about yourself, what amount of self-esteem you are led to have by your society, what your society tells you about the opportunities that are likely to be open to you, and so on' (Nussbaum interviewed in Pyle, 1999: 244–5). Lilian Rubin (1976: 211), in her study of working class lives in the USA, writes about this issue of adapted preferences by saying that people are socialized to their appropriate roles and station in life and that the process by which this occurs 'is so subtle that it is internalized and passed from parents to children by adults who honestly believe that they are acting out choices they have made in their own life time'. Rao and Walton (2004: 15) use the concept of 'constraining preferences', by which they mean an internalization of the possibility of success or failure which then becomes transformed into individualized aspirations or expectations and comes to be seen as an objective structure of chances in life. For example, the culturally marginal place of working class students in higher education might result in self-evaluations of inadequacy that distort what they believe themselves to be capable of, so that they come to locate the problem in themselves and the belief that they are not capable of thinking intelligently or that what they have to say is not important. For example, Janet locates the problem of not achieving well in herself, saying, 'I've got a lack of confidence [in getting good grades]. Perhaps I won't do as well as everyone else, even though I have done in the past. I don't know why, I just seem to lack that confidence' (interview, 18 May 2002).

In England, gender and social class are still persistent determinants of preferences, choices and learner biographies, educational opportunities, and winners and losers (see Ball *et al.*, 2000a; Plummer, 2000; Connor, 2001; Walkerdine *et al.*, 2001; Ball *et al.*, 2002; Jackson, 2003; Archer *et al.*, 2003, Watts and Bridges, 2003). Social class, even if rather more opaque than 20 or 30 years ago, continues to shape social identities and to influence actions and attitudes across society (Bradley, 1996). Here we have Amma, a black girl from the London area, living with her mother who works as a housekeeper and her two brothers (see Ball *et al.*, 2000a). She left school at 16 having not been targeted by the teachers at her school as bright enough to stay on into the sixth form for two further years of schooling and university entrance. Amma comments that 'no one has said nothing to me about staying. No one has encouraged me to stay or nothing, so' (quoted in Ball *et al.*, 2000: 26). Bright young working class women might find that their schools are less than supportive, as peer culture reinforces low teacher expectations. Thus Janet recounts: 'We were laughed at at school because it was like "What are you doing that for, you don't want to do any work, you just want to get a job once you've finished [GCSEs]" '. While the teachers, she says, 'they we were just like, "Well we've got to get you through your GCSEs". We had careers advisers but they weren't much help . . . On the one hand it was "You've go to do as well as you can" but on the other it was "just do your GCSEs and then get a job" '. Janet comments of her school mates that, 'they didn't seem to want to get on, there was lots of disruption and people didn't really settle down to work and then it was hard for the teachers to control classes and actually teach things' (interview, 18 May 2002). The working class girl who nonetheless still aspires to higher education and wins a place enters an institution in which her cultural values may not be valued or respected, and this will impact on her identity as a learner.

We hope for only that which we have come to believe is possible for us, the practical limits of our sense of place (Bourdieu, 2003). Now, in a sense we all do this all the time, reflecting on what we have done and what is now realistically possible for us, and to a greater or lesser extent our further choices may be constrained or open. As Bridges (2004) points out, all of our choices are made in a cultural and social context, and we all adapt. But there is a critical degree of difference between having a range of options open, knowledge about wide possibilities and confidence to choose; here adapted preferences are adaptations to opportunity. This is different from adaptation to deprivation or serious lack of opportunity, having little or no knowledge or hope of something better. These are effectively unfree choices. It is the difference between what Ball *et al.* (2000b) describe as a 'choice biography' and a 'risk biography'. This is very well captured in Watts and Bridges' (2003) report on their study of widening participation to Oxford and Cambridge universities using the capability approach. For example, they quote Bisi who had not thought of applying to Oxbridge because 'it's just a bit too beyond the actual universities people like me apply to' (2003: 3). The point surely is that made by Appiah (2005: 107) that of course none of us makes a self in any way that we choose; we 'make up selves from a tool kit of options made available by our culture and society'. We then have to ask of higher education as a cultural and social practice, what tool kit of options it is making available to *all* students so that they learn and learn to choose well.

The point here is that working class students enter higher education as carriers of risk biographies; this will influence how they construct their learner identities over time. The degree of risk will certainly not be the same for all working class students and some will also bring identity capital in the form of supportive and aspirational parents and good experiences of learning and teaching at school. Nonetheless, diverse learner biographies are an issue for pedagogy in higher education. It is especially an issue in that working class students are less likely to enter higher education equipped with the cultural and linguistic capital which traditional higher education pedagogies take for granted, and are less equipped to decode the pedagogic messages (Bourdieu and Passeron, 1977). We need always to keep in mind that a policy and institutional rhetoric about 'inclusion' and 'learning' in higher education mostly takes for granted that students have the required linguistic and cultural capital. It further assumes that they also have 'the capacity to invest it profitably – which the system presupposes and consecrates without ever expressly demanding it and without methodically transmitting it' (Bourdieu and Passeron, 1977: 99). In the face of a much more diverse student intake into higher education internationally, it is not sufficient for us to yearn for a 'pedagogic paradise of traditional education' (Bourdieu and Passeron, 1977: 100). In a statement which reminds me of the experience Rauno has with his inexperienced philosophy tutor, recounted in Chapter 4, Bourdieu and Passeron (1977: 95) further note that newly recruited teachers feel the need to demonstrate their scholarship and therefore are more inclined 'to adopt the outward signs of traditional mastery than to make the effort to adjust their teaching to the real competences of their public'. Put simply, conveying knowledge is more important than any concern for how this knowledge is communicated, received or understood. Moreover, the specialist language in which disciplinary knowledge is presented is more likely to be accessible to middle class students equipped with the requisite cultural capital. This is captured in this statement from a black working class student in Archer *et al.*'s (2003: 133) study. She says about her move into higher education, 'I think that's another culture shock in a sense, the language. It is a different language from being at college, from being at school, it is a totally different language'.

In all this, then, risk is ever present for non-traditional students. Choosing higher education is a risky business; participating and succeeding involves further negotiation of risk in pedagogical contexts and organizational life as working class students struggle to become 'Subjects of their own existence' (Touraine, 2000: 266). We might then argue that these students need to develop, and be supported pedagogically in developing, the capability of educational resilience, successfully adapting to constraints to experience success, despite risk (O'Connor, 2002: 858). We might argue further that for some students this capability is foundational to developing other important higher education capabilities like knowledge and learning dispositions. We need pedagogies which foster opportunity and success, even while recognizing that pedagogy may only be one factor in the process of resilience which is 'a response to a complex set of interactions involving persons, social context and opportunities' (Rigsby, 1994: 89, quoted in O'Connor, 2002: 856).

The social and relational dimensions
of learning

This further maps over the significance of the social dimensions of learning and connections between institutional and individual levels of analysis, and the importance of bringing into view the voices of student learners and their experiences. In a recent, very useful review essay on contemporary social theories of learning, Hughes (2004) cites Osborn *et al.* (2003) and their focus on:

> The need to understand what it is that motivates and empowers an individual to take advantage of learning opportunities available to them; to shift the focus of research concern away from the *provision* of educational opportunities, from the factors that influence the *ability* to learn and towards those that impact on the *desire* to learn.
>
> (2003: 9, authors' emphasis, quoted in Hughes, 2004: 396)

The capabilities of practical reason, affiliation and emotions point us to admitting a range of social opportunities and processes into the informational space for evaluating how well widening participation students are doing in developing their agency and well-being in and through higher education. Contemporary social learning theory, as Hughes (2004) argues, departs from learning as a matter only of individual cognition or fixed or innate individual ability or disposition to learn. Hughes describes the problems with this model of learning as follows:

> It fails to recognize an individual's wider dispositions to learning in respect of confidence, motivation, perseverance and creativity. It also fails to recognize the cultural influences of family, school, peer group, media and nation and the structural influences of 'race', class, gender, sexuality and dis/ability. It takes no account of the temporal aspects of learners' biographies in terms of change. It views the learner as a passive recipient of teacher knowledge rather than as an active co-producer of meaning.
>
> (2004: 400)

The temporal aspect of learning is critical, something Comim (2003) describes as a capability of becoming (see Chapter 2). Learning pathways are seldom linear, especially not for non-traditional students who may have less idea of what to expect from higher education, even where they may have a career goal in mind. Over a 'learning career' (Bloomer and Hodkinson, 2000) a student's capability may be both enhanced or diminished. We cannot assume an automatic trajectory of progress, learning and capability achievement. To take just one example, in her final year Janet described herself losing confidence. She was struggling with her course work and had 'lost a little bit [of confidence] in the last six months'. She explained:

> We had to choose between a dissertation and an extended essay and I've

chosen the essay because I don't think I could cope with doing a big long piece of research and then after I'd chosen the essay, everyone else on my course was doing the dissertation and I felt kind of inferior . . . I just kind of felt maybe I was taking the easy option, but . . . I've done it because I don't handle long pieces of research very well and I think I'd lost interest.

(interview, 18 May 2003)

Individual learner identities are inflected and shaped by their peers, the institution and their backgrounds, and the latter is more complicated than some notion just of 'prior learning'. Identity changes and learning dispositions are interwoven. For example, if one takes on the identity of the 'successful' learner in higher education, one's disposition to learning is then positively affected. If one is failing as a learner in higher education, as Matt was, one's disposition to learn is damaged, learning becomes out of reach and without support one turns away from the shame and humiliation of higher learning, of 'never wanting that sick feeling in my stomach again' (Janice, quoted in Reay, 2004: 37). At issue is that our dispositions to learn are socially shaped, and while all students arguably have to 'decode' how higher education works and what is expected of them, I have argued that this is somewhat harder for working class students lacking the familial and schooling codes which might assist successful transitions (Bourdieu and Passeron, 1977; Stanton-Salazar, 1997). This is well captured by law student Katie as she discusses her early experiences at university in response to my question as to how she works out the 'rules' of higher education:

Basically, it's just trial and error. The first seminar you just turn up and think, what am I expected to do? But after a couple of weeks, you work out, I've got to do this amount of work, I need to get through the seminar . . . and once you're in the swing of things then it's all right. But the first couple of seminars . . . it's a bit confusing because you're not told what you're expected to read or how much you're expected to write. You're just given this list with a problem question at the end. . . . I think well am I doing enough work or have I done too much work or is it about right. . . . some people when they did their A levels they were like, it was like university. So they're all right they know what to do, but most people, we were basically clueless.

(interview, 10 May 2002)

To enable capability development, higher education pedagogy would need to recognize and value the variety of difference and the cultural resources students bring to learning. In other words, human diversity is central to capabilities in education. Thus, elsewhere I have argued for a 'pedagogy of recognition' in higher education (Walker, 2002b). Repeated encounters, with non-recognition, misrecognition, indifference and disrespect of who one is, produces 'the hidden injuries' (Sennett and Cobb, 1972) which reduce human dignity. Working class students then risk losing rather than finding themselves in higher education. Central to a pedagogy of recognition (an equality pedagogy) are participation and integration, not shame and exclusion. Thus, suggest Nixon (1997: 136) and his colleagues, 'Human flourishing requires both "recognition" *and* "equal valuing" '. In higher education, an equality pedagogy would involve processes of the educational development of individuals in participatory and inclusive learning communities in which gaining knowledge and constructing successful learner identities went hand in hand. The capabilities approach offers a kind of scaffolding or design for equality pedagogy which can be tested and adjusted empirically. The outcome would be capability development under social conditions of learning in which widening participation students developed autonomy and agency, were able to participate in deciding their own actions, educational trajectories, goals and futures, and constructed knowledgeable, confident and assertive learner identities and voices. Matters of recognition and imaginative empathy were taken up also in the previous chapter.

An equality pedagogy would require the recognition of diverse cultural modes of expression and ways of life, not only the communicative practices of the socially privileged. 'Dispassionate' speech styles often correlate with social privilege, especially the culture of middle class white men. The speech culture of women, ethnic minorities and working class people may well differ, be more expressive, more figurative, more exuberant. As bell hooks (1994: 178) writes, reflecting on her own experiences of higher education as a black working class woman at Stanford University: 'Loudness, anger, emotional outbursts, and even something as seemingly innocent as unrestrained laughter were deemed unacceptable, vulgar disruptions of classroom social order. These traits were also associated with being a member of the lower classes'. It would mean instead, seeing diverse experiences as an important knowledge resource. As one student in Lynn Tett's (2000: 189) study of non-traditional mature students commented: 'I bring my experience of being working class and knowing that I have something to offer . . . being working class isn't just about being "deprived" '.

Democratic deliberation

Nussbaum's capabilities approach offers an attractive language for describing and evaluating higher education pedagogy. But we still need to take up the concern raised by Robeyns (2003b) who notes that we need to 'add in' other social theories to the capability approach. Depending on what social theories we add, we can come to quite divergent normative conclusions, she says, not least if we draw on theories which are racist, sexist, and so on. Notwithstanding Nussbaum's affiliation capability, the approach leaves open how relations of power might work to silence some voices in a dialogic forum. This matters for all students but arguably matters even more for working class students given the relations of power, as described by Mann (2001) in Chapter 1 and the middle class culture of higher education. Here

Iris Marion Young (2000), in her explication of democratic deliberation and deliberative democracy offers a way forward, in my view. She is as concerned as Nussbaum with self-development as a key element of [deliberative] democracy, ethics and social justice. Indeed, Young argues for self-development along lines similar to Sen's equality of capabilities, saying that to be just, society must establish the circumstances for all to learn 'and use satisfying and expansive skills. . . . to play and communicate with others and express their feelings and perspectives on social life in contexts where others can listen' (2000: 31–2). Her second aspect of justice 'consists in being able to participate in determining one's actions and the condition of one's action; it is contrary is domination' (2000: 32). She argues explicitly for attention to connectedness and the inclusion of the dependent and vulnerable through the practices of a deliberative democracy, which enables collective problem-solving by all those significantly involved in or affected by a decision, under conditions of dialogue which allow diverse perspectives and opinions to be voiced.

Moreover, such inclusive discussion must attend to social differences (for example, of social class), without forcing or expecting those who are socially or culturally different to fit into dominant norms. She explains that 'the field of struggle is not level; some groups and sectors are often at a disadvantage. Fair, open and inclusive democratic processes should attend to such disadvantage' (2000: 50). Communicative democracy 'should be grounded in everyday communicative ethics' (2000: 59), allowing for equal respect and recognition of different forms of expression and speech cultures. She further argues that deliberative democratic processes are a form of practical reasoning and hence one might suggest entirely compatible with Nussbaum's capability approach. They require norms of inclusion, equality, reasonableness, and publicity' (2000: 23). Ideally, such conditions 'promote free and equal opportunity to speak', and 'a willingness to listen, open-mindedness and a collective of diverse experiences, histories, commitments, ideals, and so on' (2000: 23). In other words, widening participation would enrich pedagogy and should not be constructed as a 'problem' needing to be solved according to dominant norms. Deliberative practices, Young says, provide 'the epistemic conditions for the collective knowledge of which proposals are most likely to promote results that are wise and just' (2000: 30). Students then stand to gain new information, hear about different experiences and review their own points of view (ideas also explored in Chapter 4). At stake is that communication, talk, dialogue is inherently embedded in pedagogy, and that Young's deliberative democracy helps us to think about those communicative practices which will enable participation and learning for all.

But her ideas further point to Flores-Crespo's (2004) argument that we need to consider three intersecting circles when we situate human capabilities in higher education: the philosophical (rationality and freedom through education); the pedagogical (enabling capabilities); and the institutional (contextual conditions). If we take these three circles into account it also moves us away from an individualistic focus and situates students in broader meso- and macro- contexts and structures of opportunity and constraint (Colley, 2003).

Young points out that democratic struggle cannot wait for perfect conditions of dialogue and debate. She argues that the disadvantaged and excluded 'cannot wait for the process to become fair, because there are often so many contending interests and issues'. They therefore 'have no alternative but to struggle for greater justice under conditions of inequality' (2000: 50). This is critical for pedagogy and for capabilities because changing pedagogies in higher education also cannot wait for perfect institutional conditions. Rather, fostering capabilities in higher education is a way to create change, to make futures and to strengthen agency. Attention to democratic deliberation foregrounds both how power works in pedagogical situations and points to how we arrive at agreed capabilities. A discourse and practice of democratic deliberation points to arguments for solidarity and the irreducible plurality of our lives as central elements in a genuine politics – how people get on and make sense together, reach agreements (or have comprehensible disagreements); in short, define their situation as a common situation, or fail to do so. This certainly resonates with Nussbaum's notion of an 'overlapping consensus among people who otherwise have very different comprehensive conceptions of the good' (2000: 5). But as a political scientist Young is especially concerned with 'ordinary democracy in action', and she offers a robust language to evaluate such processes. Young then adds to the capabilities approach and elaborates matters of process for educators concerned to build democracy in contexts of diversity, conflict and sometimes irrational hatreds in their classrooms.

Realizing what are essentially democratic aspirations in pedagogical action is far from straightforward – indeed our practical efforts are likely to be imperfect where inequalities and relations of domination still prevail. Nussbaum's theory does, however, suggest a list of three core capabilities – *practical reason, affiliation, emotions* – to ask widening participation for what?; and to judge how well we are doing in higher education pedagogy in our answers. It enables us, even along just these three dimensions – which emerge from the voices of a group of widening participation students – to recognize the ways in which higher education and pedagogy might as easily generate capability 'deprivation'. It alerts us to the ways in which education produces both equity and inequity, belonging and exclusion. The capability approach asks that we look at what widening participation students are able to be and do, according to what they value for themselves. Moreover, it is important to remember that this is a multi-dimensional list – all three capabilities matter – and even taking only these three into account makes for a demanding approach to develop an inclusive pedagogy. To these three, I would want to add something like a capability for risk and resilience, because this emerges also as significant and valuable in the lives of working class students.

Notes

1 Nussbaum's list is: Life, Bodily Health, Bodily Integrity, Senses, Imagination and Thought, Emotions, Practical Reason, Affiliation, Other Species, Play, Control over One's Environment. See Nussbaum (2000a: 78–80) for a further specification of each capability, and see Chapter 6.
2 The Widening Participation Project was funded by a grant from the University of Sheffield. It involved working with 14 volunteer first generation undergraduate Sheffield University students over two years in 2002–2003. Students were contacted with the help of the Student Representative Council and from 40 volunteers, 14 were selected to include men and women and minority ethnic students in their second year of study. Over the two years each student was interviewed individually three times; they were interviewed twice in focus groups, and met twice in whole-group workshops. They also acted as student researchers, collecting data from fellow students, and kept a diary of significant teaching and learning experiences over one week.

6
Capabilities for a Higher Education List

'Preparing for life' – that perennial, invariable task of education – must mean first and foremost cultivating the ability to live daily and at peace with uncertainty and ambivalence, with a variety of standpoints and the absence of unerring and trustworthy authorities; it must mean instilling tolerance of difference and the will to respect the right to be different; it must mean fortifying critical and self-critical faculties and the courage needed to assume responsibility for one's choices and their consequences; it must mean training the capacity for 'changing the frames' and for resisting the temptation to escape from freedom, with the anxiety of indecision it brings alongside the joy of the new and unexplored.
(Zygmunt Bauman, *Community*, 2001: 138)

This is the last of three chapters which looks at pedagogy through the lens of capability. This chapter considers selecting higher education capabilities for rationality and freedom. Bearing in mind the focus here on higher education, it is important to briefly rehearse what the central and definitive function is of universities. The formal aim of universities still centres on conserving, producing through research and disseminating through teaching and learning something we might call 'higher knowledge', embedded in disciplinary structures, dynamic traditions of enquiry and standards of excellence (see Becher and Trowler, 2001). Such knowledge is for personal growth, but also to contribute to wealth creation and an educated citizenry. A selection of content from disciplinary knowledge, its translation into course design, sequence and progression over a degree programme forms the subject curriculum. Sometimes the teaching and learning activities for the mediation and representation of this knowledge and its assessment are included in the definition of the curriculum and it is the case that the acquisition of content knowledge is shaped by the form in which it is offered (Barnett and Coate, 2005). What counts as knowledge in different disciplines and what is selected for the curriculum is not neutral; it will shift over time and may be contested, for example feminist challenges to the academic curriculum (for example,

Coate, 1999; Morley, 1999; Quinn, 2003). We could argue about whether new knowledge modes are replacing more traditional forms (see Gibbons *et al.*, 1994; Bridges, 2000), and we could debate different ways of organizing knowledge in the academy through modularization, credit accumulation and transfer, and so on. But knowledge, its intellectual coherence and robustness, still lies at the heart of what it is universities do, even if it is no longer the preserve only of universities. Even employers, Bridges (2000) argues, want to see university subjects on applicants' CVs, not just lists of key skills. While the focus in this book is not on curriculum (but see Barnett and Coate, 2005), it is on pedagogies and it is pedagogy which mediates epistemological access to knowledge and its specific mode of inquiry, more or less successfully for different students. It would arguably be an odd list of higher education capabilities which did not include 'knowledge'.

My idea now is to select capabilities and to express them as an ideal-theoretical list, not over-specified or too prescriptive, paying attention to student voices and to writers on capability. Bear in mind also that capability theorists focus on human development as a whole, education is mentioned but in very broad terms. Effectively, my purpose is to provoke dialogue amongst practitioners, managers, leaders and students about what we take to be 'quality' in standards of teaching and learning in universities, and genuinely educative (good) experiences of higher education. What might higher pedagogies, for example, look like if they adopted a capabilities framework for evaluating the quality of learning and teaching?

This chapter opens with a few brief examples to add to Chapters 4 and 5, illustrating further how pedagogy shapes student identities as learners, and fosters or constrains capabilities.

Constraining capability development

I turn first to examples which add to the widening participation voices in Chapter 5, and suggest that higher education which entrenches oppressive stereotypes through curriculum and pedagogy diminishes capability. In the first examples, gender inequalities demonstrate how capability might be reduced (or we could say unequally or unevenly distributed) in everyday, small pedagogical and communicative instances. It further demonstrates the argument (explored later in the chapter) that gender capability and education capability are indissoluble. First up is Norah, a working class student, studying English at the University of Sheffield, who said this in an interview with me:

> I was sitting there in the class with this lad and he was quite bright. And he just started going, blah, blah, blah, and I put forward a few ideas but I was very unsure. Then afterwards the tutor asked us what we thought and this lad just came out with this whole thing, like I'd never heard him say, I think he just presumed that I was completely stupid and that he'd

have to take charge of the situation himself . . . There's not many lads who study English compared to the percentage of girls, but if you have a boy in the class he will usually speak up.

(interview 29 May 2002)

This dented her confidence, Norah said, and she stopped going to seminars after this for a while. Paula Rothenberg (2000: 80) says she learnt during her undergraduate years at the University of Chicago that 'success was contingent on being one of the boys' so she 'adopted the pitbull approach to classroom discussion, attack first and think about it afterwards'. Jocey Quinn's (2003: 96) study argues that women students have yet to take over or even carve out an equal space in the learning environments of the academy where assumptions of academic value are still gendered. It is men who are expected by their lecturers to do 'exceptionally well'; for women to succeed academically 'they must mimic masculine behaviour'. In such cases, women students' full capability as rational and freely choosing agents is limited; their capability (freedom) to acquire knowledge and freely participate in learning is restrained, and their feminine identities devalued. Here is a compelling quote from one of the diaries kept by second year undergraduate students in Quinn's study, demonstrating the inequalities of power in the pedagogy described:

Had lecture this morning – male tutor.

Was enraged by lecture which was 'over the heads' of all of us and made deliberately so by ultra academic language delivered at speed which made note taking impossible. This is not education at all but arrogant display. Lecturer returned to class for seminar and asked, with smirk, whether everyone had understood. Youngest and most unsure-of-herself student said she hadn't understood a word of it. Quick rejoinder from lecturer that it was her lack of intelligence or something like that – and post colonial theory by definition went over the heads of undergraduates. I said twice that I should be included in those who hadn't understood and was completely ignored . . . I don't know what to do about this.

(quoted in Quinn, 2003: 90)

We hear in this echoes of Paula Rothenburg's (2000: 79) experiences of 'the brash young men' who taught her, 'the slightly deprecating smirk they adopted', that 'made you feel that whatever you said was simply wasting valuable class time', and the humiliation of having her undergraduate prose described as 'pointless and trite' and compared to 'a used car dealer's jargon'. As David Noble's (1992) history of universities shows, valued knowledge production and its legitimization from the outset 'was a world without women', whose effects continue into the present-day academy.

In my next example, we hear a student talking movingly about how she, as a black South African woman, experiences the teaching of her white female university lecturer; ironically the context is a degree in Speech and Hearing Therapy:

You allowed me into your training because you said I was good enough, but once in it you fail me over and over. You fail me because I cannot express myself in your language as well as the English speaking students, and I fail because I have to learn more than the words of your teaching – I have to give back to you the way you think. This is what you are really testing, this is how you assess my 'intelligence'. My failing is because I'm not a ripe coconut yet. However this failing also gives you great power over me and has kept me silent until now, the same way it has kept the many black students silent through the years of their failure. You have words that you use to keep me silent . . . You say, 'There she goes, the empty vessel – she's making a noise because she's empty.' It takes a lot of understanding to see how you failing me defends your monster from criticism from outside. It takes a lot of thinking to understand how words like these keep the monster quiet and makes her believe it is she who is wrong, and not the western monster of your profession.

(Mpumlwana, 2000: 539)

In my final example, the effects of a student's fearful struggle with learning on her being are viewed from a slightly different angle, recounted here by Jane Tompkins, a professor of English in the USA. Tompkins is making the case for university teachers as educators of whole human being, with some responsibility for the emergence of an integrated person:

I'll never forget an incident told to me by a professor of Portuguese language and literature from Umass, Amherst, a dedicated teacher who had been teaching for a long time. One day, she said, she was walking down a street in Amherst when she saw this striking woman crossing the street – the woman seemed powerful and fearless as well as beautiful. Then the professor did a double take. This was the same undergraduate who had huddled in a seat at the back of her language class all semester, never opening her mouth. My friend said she never forgot that moment – how strong and free, full of life and energy the student seemed, compared to the weak mousy person the professor had imagined her to be, because she wasn't very good at Portuguese.

(1996: 219)

If gender equality and other forms of diversity equality are implicated in distributing education capability then we need pedagogical strategies which take this up practically. Women's education, black people's education, mature students' education, all should arguably enhance agency through knowledge and skills.

Enhancing capability

Higher education which equips women and men as critical and challenging thinkers, as intelligent and active participants in learning, which engages imaginations and emotions, enhances their capability. This leads me to three further examples which demonstrate hope rather than despair. The first is taken from a problem-based learning fieldwork module in Zoology (Harland, 2002), which required students to collaborate with each other, with tutors taking on the role of facilitator-teachers. One of the students described his experiences of learning and teaching in this way:

> Group work itself can work very well, but I find it even better when there is some sort of guidance from the outside as you [the tutor] offered it in Ras Mohammad. This was not a 'leadership' imposed on us as is very often done in group work at university, but a kind of help or guidance when you were stuck. You were there for us if we needed you but you did not force upon us what seemed right for you. Very often, work at university is not a search for the truth or the right way to go, but a search for what the relevant teacher will assume is 'right' or 'true' and this is always something I had difficulties dealing with. In Egypt you showed us that you didn't know the perfect answer either; that you were looking for it as well and not waiting for us at a pre-set goal. Often there were several ways of solving a problem and the way you choose is as important as reaching the goal. Very often at university I have the feeling that to reach the one and only goal set by the teacher is the only thing that counts, but you are never taught how to actually approach the problem. But you didn't seem to wait for our failure or success (might be a harsh expression, but that's how I sometimes feel at university, not always of course. . . .) but you [tutors] were a team within our team. Seeing us from the outside, still teachers, different but not far away.
>
> (quoted in Harland, 2002: 12–13)

My next example is from Tara Brabazon (2002), an Australian academic who was the first in her family to go to university. She vividly describes her first day at university, one of 300 students crammed into a lecture theatre for a history class. The lecturer arrives:

> His name was Professor Richard Bosworth, and that title certainly suggested that he was important. The passion that he conveyed for history, teaching and students in that first lecture changed my life forever. On *that day*, I decided to be an historian. I did not really know what an historian was, but if being one contained 10 percent of the excitement I felt in that lecture, then it was enough for a lifetime . . . I remember going home that first day and looking up qualifications in the university handbook, about which I knew nothing. I decided to complete a masters degree in history.
>
> (2002: 119, author's emphasis)

My final example is historical, not contemporary, and it is about adult night school rather than higher education, but it illustrates beautifully my point about the importance of pedagogy: to student identity, to life-changing learning, to the love of acquiring knowledge and the ability to do so, in short to capability formation and our striving for freedom. It is taken from African American Zora Neale Hurston's autobiography:

> Nickeling and dimeing along was not getting me anywhere. So I went to night school in Baltimore and that did something for my soul. There I met the man who was to give me the key to certain things. In English, I was under Dwight O.W. Holmes. There is no more dynamic teacher anywhere under any skin. He radiates newness and nerve and says to your mind, 'There is something wonderful to behold just ahead. Let's go see what it is.' He is a pilgrim to the horizon. Anyway that is the way he struck me. He made the way clear. Something about his face killed the drabness and discouragement in me. I felt that the thing could be done . . . one night in the study of English poets he read Kubla Khan . . . he liquified the immortal brains of Coleridge and let the fountain flow . . . This was my world I said to myself, and I shall be in it; and surrounded by it, if it is the last thing I do on God's green dirtball.
>
> (1942: 44–5)

All these voices add to those in Chapters 4 and 5.

Selecting higher education capabilities

The selection of capabilities, or 'dimensions' (Alkire, 2001), which I now move to offer for debate is multi-dimensional, the dimensions are incommensurable, and one cannot be reduced to any of the other dimensions. This is of crucial importance. Each dimension supports the others and all are important. A multi-dimensional list further reduces the danger of the capability approach being co-opted or domesticated in higher education as a narrow approach to developing 'skills', or 'knowledge' or 'training'. In developing and implementing higher education pedagogies it would not be sufficient to select one capability from the list and work only to develop or enhance that single dimension, for example 'knowledge'. As Alkire (2001: 8) suggested in Chapter 3, dimensions of development are like the 'primary colours' and if all of any one hue were entirely missing, then our understanding of colour would be distorted. To translate this into educational terms, if learning experiences consistently excluded either 'knowledge capabilities' or 'process [learning] capabilities', then our framework of quality learning and educational development would be reduced and impoverished in some way. More knowledge capability in a multi-dimensional approach would not make up for not having developed any process capabilities.

In Chapter 3, I suggested that not all rival conceptions of education contribute to human flourishing. We might not wish to describe as higher education therefore that which reduces freedom (intrinsically important for Sen to a good society), for example, by advocating acceptance of the legitimacy only of particular versions of knowledge. The key issue to be repeated here is that higher education ought to be a process which enhances humanity, effective agency and well-being. It should not diminish lives. What I am approaching here is the notion that if certain capabilities were not present we would not have something called 'higher education'. Experiences of exclusion, misery, harassment or boredom at school or university do not, for example, foster human capabilities of agency, confidence and social relations. One of the informants in Marion Bowl's (2003: 42) study of non-traditional entrants to higher education recounts how she was bullied at school by a teacher when she was about nine years old and says 'it knocks the stuffing out of you, it sets you back maybe two or three years'. Evaluated even against the basic capability of agency, this falls short of enhancing individual freedoms. What is at issue is the freedoms in higher education that will allow capabilities to flourish. We are then able to raise questions about what kinds of pedagogies foster, and which deny capability. Equality is then understood as equality of valuable capabilities.

Even accepting my argument developed in Chapter 3 for putting content into capability (through selecting for a list), what is unresolved is still how we arrive at such a selection. Robeyns (2003b: 70–1) suggests the following five criteria for the selection of capabilities. The first is the criterion of 'explicit formulation' by which she means any list should be 'explicit, discussed and defended'. We might argue that this stage is a deliberative and participatory move in which higher education communities work out what they want on a list. We would need to include a discussion of capabilities that would be (educationally) appropriate but for which no information is available, as well as those for which there is information. This might provide some protection against adapted preferences on the one hand; on the other it might reduce the importance of public discussion. Robeyns' second criterion is 'methodological justification' which involves clarifying and scrutinizing the method that has generated the list and justifying its appropriateness. Her third is the criterion of 'sensitivity to context' by which she means taking into account audience and situation (what is now commonly described in the UK as 'user groups', for example), speaking 'the language of the debate', and avoiding 'jargon' which might alienate a prospective group. In some contexts therefore the list might be more abstract or theory-laden than in others. (Here it is not clear if she has in mind testing a list which has already been drawn up in order to revise, change or refine it, or an initial process of generating ideas, or perhaps both.) The fourth criterion is that of 'different levels of generality', which she says is related to but distinct from the third and applies to lists which are to be implemented. This involves drawing up a list in two stages, where the first stage involves an 'ideal' list and the second a more 'pragmatic', second-best list, taking actual constraints into account.

The ideal list also relates to her first criterion to include capabilities, for which there may not be information, in an ideal list because this strengthens the argument for collecting data on them and this in turn affects analysis and practice. For example, there may not be much evidence for the importance of higher education in enhancing compassionate or inclusive citizenship, or for making this any kind of priority in a valuation exercise under marketized education conditions. But there might nonetheless be a case to be made for its importance in contemporary globalized times (see for example Bates, 2005). Attention to gender equity in and through higher education might similarly not be foregrounded in some countries but we might still wish to make an argument for women's capability of active and participatory learning in an ideal list. This is then a further protection against automatically reproducing existing biases. Robeyns' final criterion is of 'exhaustion and non reduction', by which she means that the listed capabilities should include all important elements and the elements should not be reducible to each other, although there may be some overlap. For example, one would not list respect and recognition as separate capabilities but as elements of the same capability.

Robeyns' criteria are useful, and my first stage is therefore that of explicit formulation and defence, showing how I arrive at a provisional list of higher education capabilities. Taking into account selected student voices, making this account public in this book and also at conferences and seminars is part of the process of defending my selection and inviting other voices to review and contest it. This generates an ideal-theoretical list in the first instance, and no second-best 'real world' pragmatic list is offered here. But herein lies the potential for exciting participatory research to refine and review capability lists in diverse local higher education contexts. On the other hand where such participation is difficult beyond very small groups (say under marketized conditions) it may be that an ideal-theoretical list is one way to prise open closed debates, to insert new ways of thinking about teaching and learning, and to 'speak' to policy and policy-makers. My empirical applications in Chapters 4 and 5 sought to elicit student voices but also to concretize the ideas somewhat for an audience of potential user groups in higher education. Finally, an attempt is made to include all important elements and to generate capabilities which are incommensurable. The weakness in my method is the lack of deep public participation other than through selected dissemination of the ideas to academic peers, and student voices in the research process. This should be borne in mind.

Scrutinizing capability lists

My first step is to ask if we might learn something from other capability lists to see where they overlap with higher education, even though these lists encompass the whole of human development. Here I follow Sen (2004a: 79) who advises that 'we do not put ourselves against other lists that may be relevant or useful for other purposes'. I focus briefly on Nussbaum (2000a) again, together with Narayan and Petesch (2002), Robeyns (2003b) and Sabina Alkire (2002). Nussbaum (2000a), as I explored in the previous chapter, has produced a list of 10 universal capabilities. A threshold level of all the capabilities taken together is essential she argues for a life worthy of the dignity of a human being. The issue of a threshold – effectively a 'good enough' life – arises in the context of addressing the whole of human development needs, and her own political purpose in that her list is intended to have constitutional impacts. It is not my intention here to debate the issue of 'good enough' (but see Arneson, 2000) beyond saying that in the specific case of higher education, 'good enough', or adequate, or a sufficient level of capability may well be somewhat problematic. It is hard to imagine a quality higher education whose philosophy is 'good enough' for its students, as opposed to an educational commitment for each student to be the best they can or choose to be. In other words, as teachers our aim should be towards the curriculum and pedagogical conditions that enable the highest possible level of capability for each and every student we teach, leaving it up to the students (under conditions of freedom) to choose their own level of achievement. Furthermore, 'good enough' risks being translated into 'good enough for some'. I therefore do not argue for a minimum threshold in each higher education capability.

Nussbaum's list claims to be universal and cross-cultural. Failure of capability in any one aspect would be failure to live a fully human life. To return to the arguments in Chapter 5, those capabilities she identifies which might be argued as intrinsic to education are: *practical reason; affiliation; senses, imagination and thought; and emotions* (2000a: 78–80). She argues that practical reason and affiliation (which she has elsewhere also called 'sociability', see Nussbaum, 2000b) are 'architectonic (2000b: 131). She regards it as fundamentally important that all citizens ought to be able to make their own plans of life, to employ reason and reflection in doing so and to enjoy social relations. A plan of life says who I am and what my commitments are; it involves 'integrating one's purposes over time, of fitting together the different things one values' (Appiah, 2005: 13).

What needs to be emphasized again is the importance of the multi-dimensionality of capability lists (because learning is always multi-dimensional). This is well illustrated by turning to Nussbaum's own deep concern with gender equality. Her list of 10 capabilities inextricably links gender equality with education rights (Unterhalter, 2003a). Some of the capabilities on her list might be seen as encompassing both gender and education rights, for example affiliation (see Chapter 5), others as being specific to gender equality, for example bodily integrity and safety. The point to be underscored is that capabilities such as those of bodily integrity which have a deep bearing on gender equality are part of the *same* multi-dimensional list as those which have a bearing more directly on education such as senses, imagination and thought (Unterhalter, 2003a). Unterhalter (2003a: 668) explains therefore that Nussbaum's version of the capabilities approach 'does not value gender equality in education because it is instrumental to some "social" or institutional good, but because normatively gender equality and the value of education are part of the same conception of human flourishing'.

Nussbaum's gender equality capabilities such as 'bodily integrity' and 'life' require that we pay attention to the ways in which women students' education capability might be diminished by harassment in universities, even where we think we are getting the pedagogy 'right'. There are serious examples of women's safety and lives being violated in higher education, one of the worst being the murder of 14 women in 1989 at the University of Montreal.[1] To take another example, Jane Bennett (Shore, 2003) examined gender equity and violence in higher education in South Africa. Among other findings, her research established the widely accepted practice of male lecturers approaching their female students for sexual favours and that female students acquiesce as the price of being at university. Affirmative action programmes to enrol more women in non-traditional subject areas seem to have created resentment towards female students. On the other hand, Quinn (2003) argues that the women she interviewed in the UK envisaged higher education as a protected space for women – from threats of violence, from their families' demands, or as a space of transition to adulthood. These different viewpoints are not necessarily contradictory. Quinn does not argue that universities are places of gender equality. In her research she found that women, even though the majority of undergraduates in English universities, are still not higher education's archetypal learners. Women, she argues 'are still marginal territory' (2003: 148) and the paradigms of valid knowledge have not been substantially shifted. More importantly, what is highlighted is that gender equality capability (and we might add, other equalities) must be integrated with education capability in a multi-dimensional assessment, so that educational processes in higher education 'honor the history, culture, social realities, abilities, and diversity of each of us' (Lewis, 1993: 194). Nussbaum's specific naming of 'justified anger' as included in the capability of affiliation points also to the need for women in higher education being supported in and finding voices to speak back to exclusionary practices. Indeed, Magda Lewis (1993) argues that expressing legitimate anger is creative and transformative for women (and other marginalized social groups), and a source for action and change. Across different national and local contexts the weighting of each gender equality or education equality capability may well differ. Thus in some contexts, bodily integrity might be more heavily weighted than in others, as something needing urgent attention if women are to be successful learners. In fact Nussbaum (2000a) notes that discussions with women in India led her to revise her list for a greater emphasis on bodily integrity.

What we learn from Nussbaum is that we cannot separate out equality from quality dimensions in our pedagogies. The capability approach does not allow for this, and this is a real strength, in my view, in using it as a framework for examining pedagogy. The point is surely that pedagogical or institutional encounters which are suffused with any kind of threat of harassment or humiliation, inside or outside university classrooms, are not situations for effective or confident academic learning or the full development of autonomy and agency.

Deepa Narayan and Patti Petesch's (2002)[2] comprehensive research for the World Bank brings together the experiences of over 60,000 poor men and women across some 40 countries. Their concern is with poverty reduction, not just education or higher education but it is nonetheless useful to explore where if at all education or education capabilities appear in what they describe as an empowering approach to poverty reduction. From their research, they identify ten 'assets and capabilities' which poor people identify as important to increase their freedom of choice and to improve their lives (2002: 462–70). Many of these overlap with Nussbaum's list, and at least four are relevant to educational processes: *bodily integrity; emotional integrity; respect and dignity; social belonging; and imagination, information, education.* Their informants talked about the importance of freedom from physical assaults and freedom of movement. Emotional integrity involved freedom from constant fear and anxiety. Importantly, as an element of this they mention the damaging effects of 'hopelessness' on people's well-being and agency. With regard to respect, dignity and confidence, people talked about humiliation, alienation, shame, loss of self-esteem and of not believing in themselves. I explore this matter of hope later in the chapter when I take up ideas from Appadurai (2004) and Hage (2001). Poor people reported a deep need to belong and experience bonds of solidarity, trust and reciprocity with others. They identified education as important for getting good jobs, for 'taking away shame', and establishing networks of friends. Together with the other capabilities on the list, these were identified as being essential to a life of human dignity and to well-being. Moreover as understood by the participants in this study, education is both an instrumental good (getting a job) and an intrinsic good (it brings the joy of creation), and it requires and produces relationships.

Robeyns (2003b)[3] in her proposed list of 14 capabilities for gender inequality assessment mentions a number of capabilities relevant to education, namely: *education and knowledge* (having the freedom to be educated and to use and produce knowledge); *respect* (enjoying the freedom to be respected and treated with dignity); and, *social relations* (being able to be part of social networks). She is careful to point out that the capability of education should focus on more than just credentials and degrees, but must also pay attention to processes, subject choices and career aspirations which produce gender inequalities in schools and universities. She argues that a capability analysis of educational equality should go beyond statistical indicators of performance and 'investigate the gendered hurdles to educational achievements, such as sexist behaviour and sometimes even sexual harassment by teachers, gender differences in expectations and encouragement given by parents, a male-dominated class atmosphere, and so forth' (2003a: 80). At issue here in higher education would be to tease out how universities as organizations, and processes of curriculum and pedagogy, privilege and protect dominant masculine perspectives and power. Like Nussbaum, Robeyns knits together gender equality capability and education capability so that one might argue that education which does not foster gender equality is in some way lacking or failing in its aims.

Finally, in her evaluation of a literacy project in Pakistan, Alkire (2002) generates a list of capability impacts in which at least four (*empowerment, knowledge, work, relationships*) seem relevant to educational processes.[4] Overall these less tangible impacts were more important than income outcomes for the women involved in the programme. The capability of empowerment identified by women in the literacy project as of value has some features in common with the notion of autonomy. Thus the women identified the importance gained from their literacy education of being able to solve their own problems, of deciding for themselves what is good or bad, of having equality with men, and of not accepting abuse.

Higher education and lifelong learning capabilities

Turning now specifically to applications of the capability approach to higher education, Pedro Flores-Crespo (2001, 2004) has applied Sen's capability approach to higher education in Mexico to examine how one university in the region is working to expand the human freedoms that its graduates have reason to value. As he points out, there has been some attention in exploring the capability approach to basic levels of education such as literacy, but nothing on human capabilities for university graduates. He has a particular concern explored further in Flores-Crespo (2004) with critiquing human capital approaches to higher education. His interest is not in the specificity of pedagogy but in the relationship between higher education and development, and Sen's key questions, 'how much is a nation producing?' and 'how well are its people faring?'. He focuses on the instrumental role of freedom in his study, that is how rights, opportunities and entitlements contribute to expanding human freedom in general, and in particular he considers economic facilities and social opportunities.[5] He identifies a list of seven functionings, using data from a survey of graduates' socio-economic backgrounds, a questionnaire of a sample of 177 graduates, and semi-structured interviews with 28 graduates. He explored graduates' motivations in coming to university, their aspirations, and what they were now able to do as a proxy measure for then identifying valued functionings.[6] His list (2004: 6) comprises four personal achievements (or 'beings): *being able to feel self-confidence and self-reliance; being able to visualise life plans; being able to develop further abilities*; and *being able to transform commodities into valuable functionings*. He then includes three professional achievements ('doings'): *being able to acquire knowledge required in a job position; being able to look for and ask for better job opportunities*; and *being able to choose a desired job*. He found that higher education had a positive impact on graduates' functioning capabilities in general, but also found that variety in Sen's (1999) instrumental freedoms (social opportunities and economic facilities) led to varied capability. At all times he was interested in the relationship between individual functionings and social arrangements which might block further development, for example high unemployment rates among graduates. The case study university's policy to open up opportunities to less privileged young people in the region seems to have been significant in enhancing their capabilities and functionings: to attain and change jobs, to move from one region to another, and, to imagine opportunities in the social and economic context (2001: 24). His conclusion, however, is pessimistic and Flores-Crespo suggests that the university is playing a limited role in expanding the real freedoms that its graduates enjoy because of the unfreedoms in the region, which interrupt the cycle between education, economic advancement and education.

A second study which considers valued capabilities takes a very different methodological approach. In her study of the Social Work curriculum in South Africa, Vivienne Bozalek (2004) adopts a human capabilities perspective to explore the effects of institutional racism (understood as the exclusion from resources and power) on student family circumstances, and on what students said they had been prevented from doing and being. The focus here is on constraints on human flourishing for persons not categorized as 'white' in South Africa. Her primary concern is with the effects for social work practice, or put another way, the capability outcomes of social work graduates. The particular usefulness for Bozalek of the capability approach is in its approach to vulnerability as a matter not just of a lack of resources as revealed by poverty statistics, but on how people are prevented from converting these resources to desired ends. Additionally, she integrates race equality capabilities with education capabilities such that an 'adequate education' must foster equity and anti-racism. She further integrates, as Nussbaum and Robeyns do, the family and the world of work into her account of valued capabilities, weaving together the whole of a person's life across diverse domains of activity.

Apart from its compelling substantive focus, what is also of interest here is Bozalek's methodology for generating a list of capabilities. These have all been foregrounded in the students' own accounts produced for their 'Family-in-Community' assignment, an in-depth written essay on their own family histories, circumstances and community resources, and including an interview with a family member. As a compulsory piece of work which students had to pass, Bozalek explores its possible limitations carefully and explains how she negotiated access to these profiles with the students for use as her research data. Students were under no obligation to give their permission for the profiles to be used in her research and some did not agree to this. What is at issue here is that the capabilities are generated bottom-up as it were, although it is also true to say that the student profiles are then interpreted theoretically by Bozalek through the capability lens, and that overall the research process was not particularly participatory. On the other hand there is no suggestion that she sees this list as canonical or even to be used in any other way. It is specific to the lives and circumstances of these students. By considering what students had been prevented from doing and being, Bozalek produces a list of 15 capabilities valued by her students, and provides a detailed account from her data to show how each of the 15 capabilities has been derived.[7] The list includes: *being able to move from place to place; being able to live for and to others; being able to work as a human being,* and *being able to imagine, to think, and to reason in a way informed and cultivated by an adequate education.* Students wrote, for example, about the unfairness and discrimination that had excluded their family members on racist grounds from educational opportunities. Her curriculum concern arising from this account is that social work texts used in undergraduate programmes construct the lives of the poor or racially excluded as pathological and deviant. These texts teach students that their own histories are pathological and deviant, and that they and any similar families they might encounter as social workers are hence to be judged as lacking. Instead, students' understandings of the effects of institutional racism on their lives and their capabilities to function as full human beings, she argues, 'have the potential to subvert traditional ways of conceptualising child and family care in the social work curriculum' (2004: 132). She argues that a social worker who recognizes the socio-political location of family practices will arrive at rather different understandings for professional practice than one who does not. Thus she writes:

> It is my contention that the human capabilities approach is particularly useful for identifying, assessing and acting upon the many forms of exclusion to which [social work] clients are exposed. This is because it goes beyond assessment of needs based upon a lack of resources. It focuses upon the social positioning of those whose needs are being assessed and allows social work practitioners to pay special attention to what would be required to achieve full human capabilities.
>
> (2004: 178)

Bozalek's concern for professional outcomes opens up the question of whether the capability approach is an opportunity or outcome-based theory of justice (Robeyns, 2003a). Sen's emphasis on personal choice makes the approach opportunity-based, but as noted previously, in professional education one is concerned with professional functioning as much as professional capability. For example, a social work student may have the capability for acting in a caring and compassionate manner. As social work educators, would we really not be concerned if the student chose not to bother in her professional work? It further returns us to the difficulty of evaluating capabilities as potential beings and doings which are not directly observable. At stake in the specific sphere of education is whether it is sufficient to focus on opportunities to function and not also on actual outcomes, that is, on functioning. Moreover we generally have to measure capability using the proxy of functioning, although Gaspar and Van Staveren (2003: 148) suggest that this is 'fortunate' for we need, they argue, to measure functionings as well as capability 'if we are to evaluate human development adequately'. Indeed, Bozalek generates valued capabilities from the student accounts on the basis that these are ways in which students are unable to function, or to function fully, for example not being able to move around freely. Lacking this functioning, we can assume points to a lack of the desired capability.

Although not identified by Bozalek herself as an explicit capability, I would argue that the capability of *aspiration and hope* is implied in her capability of 'adequate education' as a valued capability for her social work students. She quotes one of the students who wrote in her *Family Profile* that her parents had not been educated but her father had resolved when his children were born, that they would get the education he had been denied. This student wrote that, 'He believed that if he gives his children education, the pain of the past can be relieved' (quoted in Bozalek, 2004: 117). In other words, hope and aspiration for a better future is significant, and that hope is contained in education. This points me towards aspiration and hope as key capacities in Appadurai's (2004) argument for why culture matters for development and the reduction of poverty. Now, again, access and participation in higher education is well beyond direct poverty reduction, but this is not to say it is not important in developed and developing countries. Indeed, Nussbaum argues that in developing countries university-educated women are most likely to influence development debates (Record, 2003). Higher education is of course a social and cultural practice; it therefore makes sense to pay attention to Appadurai's argument. Put simply he argues that the capacity to aspire, conceived as a cultural capacity, is future-oriented and offers a resource to contest exclusions of the past and the present. It presents alternative futures and possibilities, it brings the future back in. This resonates with Hage's (2001) argument for the significance of hope. He (2001: 3) explains that hope 'is not related to an income level. It is about the sense of possibility that life can offer. Its enemy is a sense of entrapment not a sense of poverty'. Appadurai emphasizes that our capability to aspire is formed in and through our social interactions, with others, and it is not evenly distributed throughout society with the rich and powerful invariably having more and having a 'thicker' map of aspirational nodes and pathways. He declares that:

> It means the better off you are (in terms of power, dignity, and material resources), the more likely you are to be conscious of the links between the more and less immediate objects of aspiration . . . The more privileged in any society simply have used the map of its norms to explore the future more frequently and more realistically and to share this knowledge with one another more routinely than their poorer or weaker neighbours.
>
> (2004: 68–9)

The capability to aspire thrives on being practised, that is, functioning cannot be overlooked. It is crucial for the poor, or in my case, students in higher education to function aspirationally. Appadurai argues that aspiration 'thrives and survives on practice, repetition, exploration, conjecture and refutation' (2004: 69). It moves this capacity from being wishful thinking to 'thoughtful wishing' (2004: 82). He links the capacity to aspire to voice, arguing that each accelerates and nurtures the other. Thus, 'it is through the exercise of voice that the sinews of aspiration as a cultural capacity are built and strengthened, and conversely, it is through exercising the capacity to aspire that the exercise of voice by the poor will be extended' (2004: 83). Where higher education fosters voice, here understood as the capacity to debate, contest, inquire and participate critically, it simultaneously nurtures aspiration. As Bernstein (2000: 12) says, 'To know whose voice is speaking is the beginning of one's own voice'. Where students might be denied a cap-ability for voice in the home or in society, or where their aspirations might be cramped outside of higher education, there is then a particular ethical responsibility placed on universities to challenge exclusion, not to perpetu-ate it.

Crucially, Appadurai says aspiration is a 'navigational' capacity, a kind of 'personal life-project' (Touraine, 2000: 13) in which we are able to construct a coherent individual life story in a changing world. The importance of such a capacity is underlined by research in post-school education in the Life Patterns project, a study of young Australians from the State of Victoria in Australia, who left school in 1991. The project has found that the ability to navigate one's way through uncertain contemporary times, that is the role that choice and decision-making play in young people's lives, is critical for agency and well being (Wynn, 2004). We have to negotiate our own lives more reflexively, to change and adapt, under contemporary conditions in developed countries of a knowledge economy and post-industrial order (Giddens, 1991; Field, 2000; Edwards *et al.*, 2002). Johanna Wynn (2004) points out that in evaluating education and the quality of education we need to consider social, subjective and attitudinal factors as much as economic forces. In other words, research such as Wynn's in Australia highlights again the problem of decoupling economic success from a sense of well-being. She argues that the young people in the study have learned that their own per-sonal development, adaptability and capability to make the 'right choices' are the most important resources for building their own lives. She suggests that this pressure on individuals to shape their own pathways through educa-tion and into employment 'favours identities that are based around their own capabilities and personal autonomy' (2004: 15). They are, she says, 'navigators of their own biographies and careers' (2004: 17).

This is further borne out by John Field (2000) who in his critical work on lifelong education in Europe, suggests that in a 'risk society' (Beck, 1992) we all face discontinuities through our life course through which we must make our way. Edwards *et al.* (2002) present an argument for reflexivity as central to lifelong learning in the context of such uncertainties, and an argument relevant to higher education. Their arguments resonate, for example, with the Harvard commitment to 'a lifetime of learning' (2004: 6), and to educat-ing 'reflective thinkers' (2004: 1) and 'intellectually acute citizens of the world' (2004: 8). Edwards *et al.* argue for a notion of learning that involves more than simply passively acquiring skills and qualifications, 'one more consonant with the needs of civic participation and of agents capable of autonomously generating change for themselves' (2002: 527). This they say, requires 'reflexivity' – 'self and social questioning (reflexivity) that people are able to engage with and (en)counter – be affected by but also affect – contemporary uncertainties' (2002: 527). This clearly has elements in common with Nussbaum's practical reason and Barnett's (1997) 'critical being'. They remind us that change processes are experienced differentially, patterns of participation in learning through life vary, and that one should not assume the 'freely choosing individual and family' of lifelong learning policy. Importantly they highlight learning, arguably the heart of education at any level. They describe learning as:

> the transformation of understanding, identity and agency . . . involving a developing awareness which results in growing understanding of customary practice, leading to reflexive social and self-questioning and the transformation of 'habitus'. It is the development of reflexivity, the capacity to develop critical awareness of the assumptions that underlie practices, especially the meta-cognitive, interpretative schema that constitute worlds, which we see as central to an adequate theory of lifelong learning . . . the capacity to develop and sustain reflexivity.
>
> (2002: 532–3)

We develop such reflexivity and dispositions to learn in the context of actual practices, activities and learning relationships in situated socio-cultural, institutional and historical contexts. Crucially they insert the importance of knowledge as key for a *critical* reflexivity. Disciplinary boundaries and curricular knowledge selections are at the heart of learning and learning cultures in higher education and the core epistemological function of a university – we learn something (history, philosophy, engineering, physics) as much as we learn how to be (see Becher and Trowler, 2001).

From the perspective of lifelong learning, we should also have in mind Comim's (2003) argument about the importance of time and hence of becoming, as well as being and doing in the capability approach, together with Biggeri *et al.*'s (2004) similar point that different ages may give different importance to valued capabilities. When we talk about education we usually have in mind that some kind of learning takes place. But learning is seldom linear and immediate; it is more often recursive, new learning builds on existing knowledge, past experience and student identities. Learning is then a process of becoming as well as being a person over a life course, and through cycles of education. We might measure capability by some means or other through learning at a point in time using a specific assessment tool. But at another point that same capability might look different and the learning therefore be more or less successful, deep or sustainable than previously, with effects for an individual's learning disposition. For example, a student might be a successful mathematics learner in the secondary school, only to encounter difficulties with the subject or its teaching in higher education such that earlier learning and her learning identity is undermined and instead of progressing further she either gives up mathematics altogether or does progressively worse and worse in tests and examinations. Development is necessarily dynamic and expansive so that we need to extend the capability informational space to take account of this. This is not to say that we cannot analytically freeze a point in time of learning and voices of, in and on learning, but we should keep in mind that as a process of development, education will shift and change over time.

Following the Harvard concern with world citizenship, and Nussbaum's (see Chapter 1) argument for cosmopolitanism, we might elaborate the capabilities of *respect, dignity and recognition* mentioned earlier, and link them to responsible citizenship and political judgement by turning to Hannah Arendt's (1977: 196) emphasis on the importance of the capability of judgement which she sees as central to preparing young people through education 'for the task of renewing the common world'. For Arendt judgement is linked to imagination, affiliation and reflection – being able to imagine what the world looks like from the perspective of others, thus enabling an 'enlarged mentality'. In turn this capacity requires critical thinking and plurality – exposing one's own ideas to those of others. Arendt describes this as 'being and thinking in my own identity where actually I am not' (1977: 241–2), disinterestedly taking into account the standpoints of others while thinking through an issue, imagining how one would feel and think in their places, and so strengthening the quality of judgement arrived at. For Arendt imagination is then *educationally* crucial, and crucial for critical thinking and applying critical standards to one's own ideas – as she puts it, we train our imaginations 'to go visiting'. We weave together equality, education and capability with social relations and a politics of dignity and recognition (Appadurai, 2004). This is crucial if the capability approach is not to be domesticated or interpreted as a highly individualized approach which might serve to legitimize inequality in more individualized societies where well-being or participation in education is understood to be a matter of individualized choice, and individualized success or failure (Field, 2000). It assumes a richer picture of what it means to be a person and what it means to be educated in and through higher education.

At this point it is important to reiterate the importance the capability theorists and researchers discussed earlier place on *social relationships* with people for agency and well-being, Appadurai's emphasis that aspiration is a capacity acquired interactively and socially, and the stress in Edwards *et al.*'s (2002) theory of learning on learning relationships. We could take this further and argue that a just society is something that we make together, by thinking and working with others so that freedom is constructed in-between. Following Arendt, Maxine Greene and Morwenna Griffiths (2003: 83) argue that freedom 'is to be found in action *with* others. It is not simply the negative freedom of interference *from* others, nor again is it simply the freedom to make individual choices' (authors' emphasis).

An ideal-theoretical list for capability distribution and evaluation

Taking the ideas from capability theorists, student voices and researchers and selected relevant research in higher education and lifelong learning into account, we might have a draft ideal-theoretical, multi-dimensional education list something like this. It demonstrates an argument and method and is in no way fixed, although it might offer a starting point for discussion about the capability approach and teaching and learning in higher education.

Here capabilities are understood both as opportunities but also as skills and capacities that can be fostered (Gaspar and Van Staveren, 2003), in higher education:

1. *Practical reason.* Being able to make well-reasoned, informed, critical, independent, intellectually acute, socially responsible, and reflective choices. Being able to construct a personal life project in an uncertain world. Having good judgement.
2. *Educational resilience* Able to navigate study, work and life. Able to negotiate risk, to persevere academically, to be responsive to educational opportunities and adaptive to constraints. Self-reliant. Having aspirations and hopes for a good future.
3. *Knowledge and imagination.* Being able to gain knowledge of a chosen subject – disciplinary and/or professional – its form of academic inquiry and standards. Being able to use critical thinking and imagination to comprehend the perspectives of multiple others and to form impartial judgements. Being able to debate complex issues. Being able to acquire knowledge for pleasure and personal development, for career and economic opportunities, for political, cultural and social action and participation in the world. Awareness of ethical debates and moral issues. Open-mindedness. Knowledge to understand science and technology in public policy.
4. *Learning disposition.* Being able to have curiosity and a desire for learning. Having confidence in one's ability to learn. Being an active inquirer.
5. *Social relations and social networks.* Being able to participate in a group for learning, working with others to solve problems and tasks. Being able to work with others to form effective or good groups for collaborative and participatory learning. Being able to form networks of friendship and belonging for learning support and leisure. Mutual trust.
6. *Respect, dignity and recognition.* Being able to have respect for oneself and for and from others, being treated with dignity, not being diminished or devalued because of one's gender, social class, religion or race, valuing other languages, other religions and spiritual practices and human diversity. Being able to show empathy, compassion, fairness and generosity, listening to and considering other person's points of view in dialogue and debate. Being able to act inclusively and being able to respond to human need. Having competence in inter-cultural communication. Having a

voice to participate effectively in learning; a voice to speak out, to debate and persuade; to be able to listen.
7. *Emotional integrity, emotions.* Not being subject to anxiety or fear which diminishes learning. Being able to develop emotions for imagination, understanding, empathy, awareness and discernment.
8. *Bodily integrity.* Safety and freedom from all forms of physical and verbal harassment in the higher education environment.

The detail in this list could be argued to be too prescriptive. But I would emphasize again that I am demonstrating a method. Still, we could argue that a basic core selection is a better starting point for discussion: *Practical reason; Educational resilience; Knowledge and imagination; Learning disposition; Social relations and social networks; Respect, dignity and recognition; Emotional integrity and emotions; Bodily integrity.* It is important nevertheless to remember that any selection is multi-dimensional; each capability influences and shapes the development of others.

There are elements not included on this core list which others might see as essential – for example 'play' and 'aesthetic senses'. There is nothing here directly about the capability for political participation as a democratic citizen, although it is certainly implied, or about care for the environment. There are elements elaborated as part of my list which others might prefer to name as a core capability, for example 'creativity' or 'inter-cultural communication'. Some might wish to foreground the capability of oral and written communication as core elements. I have used the language of 'respect' in my list, but others might prefer Nussbaum's (2000a) idea of 'affiliation'. Such matters are best discussed and decided in specific higher education communities. But we should always keep in mind that the capability approach: (i) incorporates both rationality and freedom; (ii) it is for equality and quality; (iii) it is for complexity and for multi-dimensionality, not single capabilities; (iv) it is for educational development; (iv) and, above all for agency – constructing oneself as an actor – and well-being. It is therefore against this broader framework – perhaps translated into working questions – that any specific selection should be developed.

As a final step we would need to consider what information we need to evaluate these capabilities. This might include statistical indicators on resource inputs, class sizes, library spend, progression data in different subjects, degree results and degree classes, diversity indicators, and so on. But it would also need to include, in my view, the voices and narratives of students, university teachers and others involved in and affected by teaching and learning in order to ascertain their experiences, demands, preoccupations, and relationships (Touraine, 2000), and what they value in and from their learning.[8] This issue of measurement remains undeveloped in the capability approach and constitutes a key challenge for taking it forward (Robeyns, 2003b).

This selection draws on a quasi-anthropological exercise in Chapters 4 and 5, but it is nonetheless more an ideal-theoretical exercise. Nevertheless, as my argument in Chapter 3 demonstrated, we need some kind of selection. I am arguing that in higher education we are distributing capabilities, and that there are capabilities which are specifically educational, such that if they were not being encouraged we might have reason to question whether a process of higher education was under way. I have argued that there are already capabilities relevant to education in the capability approach and relevant to asking 'equality of what' in the sphere of education. My ideal theoretical exercise shows what might be included in such a list. It does not attempt any valuation weighting, although it does argue that the list is multi-dimensional and all dimensions are important for evaluating higher education using a criterion of justice. From the perspective of pedagogies, we might then ask who has the power to develop valued education capabilities, and who has not? We might wish to check (measure) how successful students are in bringing about what they are trying to achieve. Finally, if there is unevenness, patchiness and inequality in learners' well-being freedom and agency freedom we might wish to raise political and ethical questions about the society in which some adults can promote all their ends while others face barriers, whether of social class, race, gender, culture or disability.

Pedagogy through a capability lens

What evaluative picture would emerge if we were to take all examples of student voices, obviously neither detailed nor exhaustive but representative for all that, and consider them in the light of human capabilities? At issue is that how important higher education capabilities are distributed in the examples earlier and in Chapters 4 and 5, points practically to in/equality in higher education and hence to strategies for action and change. We need *both* critique *and* change. I am reminded here of a story from the Peanuts cartoon characters story recounted by Clifford Geertz (2000: 24). As Geertz tells it, Lucy says to Charlie Brown: 'You know what the trouble is with you Charlie Brown? The trouble is you're you' ... Charlie Brown asks: 'Well whatever can I do about that?' and Lucy replies: 'I don't give advice. I just point to the roots of the problem.' The point is that in education we ought to try to connect such research to practical attempts to improve higher education. In education and human development, what is at stake is *both* the roots *and* the replanting and a kind of cyclical, action-based 'reflective equilibrium' (Nussbaum, 2000a; Rawls, 2001) in which our research and theorizing speak to practice and change, and practice and change talk back to research. Thus I would further argue that capabilities also provide a set of ideas to take up practically to develop higher education pedagogy according to a criterion of justice, to which I now turn.

Notes

1 On 6 December 1989, Marc Lepine walked into an engineering classroom at the University of Montreal and methodically shot 14 women, taking aim first at women and then only at (four) men who interfered. He separated the women from the men (who went along with this), shouting 'You are all feminists, I hate feminists'. One of the young survivors recounted how she pleaded 'we are only women in engineering who want to live a normal life' (Lakeman, 1989: 1).

2 Narayan and Petesch's list is: Material assets, Bodily health, Bodily integrity, Emotional integrity, Respect and dignity, Social belonging, Cultural identity, Imagination, information and education, Organizational capacity, Political representation and accountability.

3 Robeyns' full list is: Life and physical health, Mental well-being, Bodily integrity and safety, Social relations, Political empowerment, Education and knowledge, Domestic work and nonmarket care, Paid work and other projects, Shelter and environment, Mobility, Leisure activities, Time-autonomy, Respect, Religion.

4 From the literacy project, in dialogue with the capability approach, Alkire produces this list: Empowerment, Knowledge, Work, Life/health/security, Relationships, Inner peace, Religion.

5 The former is described by Sen (1999: 40) as 'the opportunities that individuals respectively enjoy to utilize economic resources for the purpose of consumption, production, or exchange' and the latter as 'the arrangements that society makes for education, health care and so on, which influence the individuals substantive freedom to live better'. Following Sen, Flores-Crespo considers monetary benefits as a means of development, not its end, and the complementarity of individual agency and social arrangements.

6 In an earlier paper (2001: 9), Flores-Crespo described the proposed functionings as: being able to emigrate; being able to acquire knowledge and certification; being able to change jobs (and consequently to receive fair payments); being able to define a life plan; being able to have social and labour opportunities in the region; being able to feel self-confidence and self-reliance; being able to have extra resources to transform commodities into functionings.

7 Bozalek's 15 capabilities are: being able to move from place to place; having freedom from unwarranted search and seizure; being able to control one's own life in one's own surroundings and context; being able to experience and produce spiritually enriching religious events of one's choice; being able to live for and in relation to animals, plants and the world of nature; being able to have attachments to things and persons outside ourselves; to have adequate shelter; to have the right to equal employment on an equal basis with others; in work being able to work as a human being, exercising practical reason and entering into meaningful relationships of mutual recognition with other workers; being able to imagine, to think, and to reason in a way informed and cultivated by an adequate education; being able to live to the end of a human life of normal length; to be adequately nourished; being able to laugh, play; to enjoy recreational activities; and, freedom of association.

8 See Alkire (2002) on adult literacy capability evaluation for a possible methodological approach to measurement. Also see Unterhalter and Brighouse (2003) for one attempt to develop a set of capability indicators for gender equality, and Robeyns (2005) for a theoretical approach to measurement.

Part 4

Change in Higher Education

7
Pedagogy, Capabilities and a Criterion of Justice

...a society's education entails (in all senses) its future. To allow the utopian imagination to become so stunted that the practices and contents of teaching carry no message to the future about its emancipation, nor hold out in Stendahl's great phrase, a promise of happiness, is only to ensure that the future society will be an awful one.

(Fred Inglis, *Education and the Good Society*, 2004: 4)

This final chapter draws together the ideas explored through this book into making the case for the capability approach as the basis for pedagogy which points to a criterion of justice in higher education.

University teaching and capabilities

Before I attempt to rehearse the main points for the capability approach I wish to turn briefly to the voices of university teachers, the other half of the teaching-learning dyad.

Undoubtedly across the world universities pressure academic staff to research and publish; it is probably fair to say this is the most prestigious and generally best rewarded activity in terms of academic status in higher education. It is not my intention to engage this issue, nor the debates about the relationship of research to good teaching (but see Rowland, 1996; Elton, 2001; Jenkins 2000). I simply note it here in order to move on to also saying that undergraduate teaching – and indeed quality post-graduate teaching and supervision – undoubtedly *does* matter to students, and university teaching potentially influences their development. For example, based on his 10 years of interviews with staff and students at Harvard University, Richard Light states that:

> When asked to estimate their own impact on students, more than a few of my faculty colleagues rate it as 'modest'. Perhaps for some professors

this perception is correct. Yet for others it couldn't be more wrong. According to undergraduates, certain professors exert a profound impact. They influence students' development as young scholars, as good citizens, as human beings.

(2001: 104)

Teaching voices

My selection of capabilities focused on the learning of students, but we would need also to find out what capabilities teachers see as valuable, because what university teachers do pedagogically potentially influences the development of their students. For example, Judy Wilkinson, a lecturer in engineering, argues that:

How we teach reflects our respect for the students, our commitment to the academic community and our responsibility for the world . . . Our commitment to our community entails inculcating in the students an enjoyment of 'the pursuit of difficulty' so that they reach the highest intellectual level of which they are capable. Responsibility to the world means developing, with students, critical and reflective tools so that they can discuss and act, with authority, on the dominant political issues which affect their lives.

(2001: 167)

I want briefly now to take just one illustrative example which points in the direction of a method of lecturer voice in selecting teaching and learning capabilities. I interviewed Sarah Dowling, a lecturer in modern languages, for around two hours on 19 November 2002.[1] My discussion with her suggests four valuable capabilities as process and outcomes of her pedagogy. The first is that of *critical knowledge and open-mindedness*. She wants her students to be proficient in French and to know about its literature. But more than this she wants them 'to criticise' and 'to grow as thinking beings', to have 'open minds, not shut minds, to whatever they're going to encounter'. Her second capability is for students to find their own *critical and independent voices*. Thus she asks them in the context of literary criticism not only 'where is the narrator's voice?', but also 'where is your voice?', finding ways to work peda-gogically over time to support students to recognize their own voices and not just 'speak my voice back to me'. It is not just any old voice she seeks to encourage, but a critical voice. 'They will disagree with each other in front of you', she says, when her approach works well. 'They won't just give the answer they think you want to hear, they will actually engage, talk across each other, they're beginning to form their own point of view'. But this develop-ment should also be based in constructive dialogue and disagreement, and always with the third capability of '*respect for other people*'. Finally her fourth capability is for her students '*to learn to communicate and relate to each other*' because 'we grow in relationships with other people'. Crucially, Sarah's own educational aims and purposes to 'value who your students are as people, each and every student, as human beings' are deeply intertwined with her students' capability development, in other words she needs to develop her own professional capability in order to support student learning. For example, she comments reflexively that the capability of voice is complex, and not to be mandated:

> . . . there's no law that says that at the age of 20 you will start to develop your own voice. For many of them, that may come much later and they are at a transition stage . . . talking in a mixture of voices and borrowed voices, and that is OK. I mean I don't have the right to dictate how they will develop, I do have the responsibility to show them the importance of development and help them to develop . . . Those who won't, I think again you have to respect the fact that they won't.

Very quickly, I want also again to mention the Harvard University Curricular Review (2004) because this also points to the concerns of university teachers and what this particular group identify as valuable beings and doings. Other university teachers in other places might articulate their aims differently, or prioritize their concerns differently. This is not the point. Rather, the issue is to suggest how educational aims might be expressed as capabilities. The Harvard review notes a number of educational aims for undergraduate education, which we might describe as capabilities. These aims include: students as reflective, disciplined and independent thinkers; having multiple perspectives on the world; becoming responsible human beings and citizens; as knowledgeable and creative thinkers; as intellectually acute citizens of the world; able to grapple with scientific and technological elements of public policy and ethical questions; able to participate in communities of learning; able to write clearly and effectively as a tool for communication; ability to speak cogently and persuade others; having quantitative skills; and aware of moral and ethical debates and questions.

Professionalism and accomplished university teaching

Now, because pedagogy is relational and interactional, we as lecturers also change and are changed by our encounters with students. Because our own academic and personal values shape the pedagogical decisions we make, even where we are constrained by contemporary policy and organizational climates, we ought to work at developing our own professional judgement. As Sarah suggests, while we cannot teach development to our students, we can establish the conditions under which such development might flourish. It then follows that as university teachers our task 'is that of constructing a range of situations where the critical life in all its demands . . . can be sustained' (Barnett, 1997: 164). The point here is that fostering student capabilities simultaneously requires our own reflexive professional learning and a renewed academic professionalism consistent with Said's (1994: 62) argument for a professionalism based not on 'doing what one is supposed to do', but on asking 'why one does it, who benefits from it, how it can connect with a personal project and original thoughts'. This requires in pedagogy, a 'situational ethical' (Bagnall, 2002: 79), sensitive to the particularities of pedagogical events. Bagnall's (2002) elaboration of ethical action that flows from a situational ethic might be the first stage in developing a professional capabilities list. He writes as follows:

> Ethical action so understood is characterised by: a reflexive awareness of one's own cultural being, location and impact; a humility with respect to the importance of one's own framework of beliefs; a tolerance of and respect for otherness; an empathic understanding of and responsive-ness to the particularities of other's lived realities; the capabilities, understanding and dispositions involved in successfully negotiating understandings with others; and the acceptance of responsibility for one's beliefs, actions and consequences.
>
> (2002: 79)

As university teachers we would be concerned both with educational pro-cesses and with educational outcomes. We would teach to the end of helping others to learn.

We might describe these ideas as pedagogical or teaching standards by which we normatively judge teaching and learning. But these would be radically different from dominant notions of performance indicators. The difference is captured by lecturer in hispanic studies Mike Gonzalez, a par-ticipant in the 'Critical Professionalism' project at the University of Glasgow (Walker, 2001a). He addresses the question, what is effective teaching, which he argues could be answered in two different ways. One answer is to say that effective teaching 'more efficiently produces the functional ends to which the institution is dedicated and therefore renders it more efficient, more effective, more cost beneficial' (quoted in Walker, 2001a: 19). But, says Gonzalez, another response might be:

> an altogether less tangible purpose which is to more effectively encour-age a critical response to the world by individuals and groups of people, whose outcome is not easily quantifiable or measurable or functional, except in a broader sense of making people richer, fuller in their engagement with the world ... The real benefit, the most profound benefit, for the students, is discovering how to discover the world, how to ask and answer questions about the world and how to do it with other people ...
>
> (quoted in Walker, 2001a: 19)

Such capabilities might then frame accomplished teaching and standards for professional practice in higher education. Here I deliberately use the lan-guage of accomplished rather than 'excellent' or 'effective' teaching in order to avoid two words which have become increasingly hollow and mean-ingless and fused with the discourse of the corporate university and an accounting culture (Readings, 1996). As Readings (1996: 39) points out, an appeal to excellence 'marks the fact that there is no longer any idea of the University, or rather that the idea has now lost all content'. We might say something similar about the notion of 'quality' and 'quality assurance' in teaching and learning which may say very little about actual practice and learning and more about measurability, efficiency, customer quietude and representation (Morley, 2003). It says little, if anything, about professional responsibility. I do not therefore have in mind the notion of standards which are appropriate for identifying 'excellence in teaching', as Elton and Partington (1993) propose. Rather, I have in mind participatory and dialogic higher education communities selecting capabilities for learning and teaching, and using these as a framework of standards for evaluating accomplished professional practice. Such professional standards would recognize the complex nature of university teaching because the capability approach is multi-dimensional. It would then be interesting, for example, to take my ideal-theoretical list of selected capabilities and think through the implications for teaching capability.

The point here would be to ask what university teaching would look like if evaluated against a multi-dimensional grid of capabilities, arrived at through a participatory process by those affected by higher education teaching and learning, and minimally involving lecturers and students.

Capabilities, and higher education pedagogies

The book has presented an argument for higher education pedagogies to be grounded theoretically in Sen's and Nussbaum's capability approach – valued beings and doings – and practically in the situational production, implementation and evaluation of selected 'teaching and learning' capabilities. The first chapter explained why a criterion of justice in higher education is important. I outlined the central idea Sen advocates of evaluating human development not primarily in terms of income and resource inputs, but as capability and functioning, that is of individual beings and doings in order to choose a life of value. Central to the approach is the importance of agency opportunities and achievements in choosing and leading a 'good' life. In this, individual chances and decisions are institutionally and socially shaped and influenced, and human diversity is made integral in our need to assess how diverse persons are able to convert resources into capabilities and functionings. Social (educational) constraints on choice and what we take to be possible for ourselves are then an issue in our development efforts.

Translated into the higher education context, the capability approach aims at freedom, human flourishing and dignity, as well as economic opportunities. It is an argument for capabilities which does not ignore economics. As Mala Singh (2003) suggests in addressing the issue of the 'engaged university', it should be possible to ask whether a university is enabling students *both* to gain the knowledge, skills and understandings required by them to maximize their freedom as job-seekers, *and* for their development as individual personalities, as confident citizens of their own countries, and as informed global citizens.

I have developed an argument for selecting higher education capabilities, arguing for a moderate perfectionism following Brighouse (forthcoming). The basic claim here is that not everything counts as higher education or higher learning and we cannot leave the matter of capabilities in the case of education and higher education entirely open. The further argument is that higher education affects our continuing journey through adult life. It then follows that the opportunities we open up or foreclose in higher education for students' capability development as ethical persons, having 'the competence to act in the world and the judgement to do so wisely' (Colby *et al.*, 2003: 7), matter. If we value democratic political deliberation, then universities, as Englund (2002) and Nussbaum (2002) say, have a responsibility to foster the values and capabilities that support democratic life.

The capability approach crucially links (educational) capability development to freedom, and complements a 'rights' language. This is absolutely fundamental in resisting a domestication or normalization of the approach. To take one example, Dennis Carlson (1995), talks about how portfolio assessment provides a way for students to reflect on their learning and to decide on the directions they want their learning to take. In other words it is potentially a progressive approach to learning. But, he argues, when it is institutionalized within a normalizing institutional discourse, its potential is unlikely to be realized. I would argue that if we took this one example, or practice, and mapped it over a grid of capabilities, we may well still struggle to realize progressive pedagogic possibilities, but we would at the same time be equipped with a language and practice to evaluate and resist these normalizing effects. The point is always, as noted in Chapter 4, that a progressive pedagogy will have to deal with ambiguities, contradictions and tensions. If an evaluation of higher education capabilities took into account Bernstein's (2000) three key pedagogic rights: the right to enhancement (the right to critical understanding and to new possibilities), the right to inclusion and the right to participation, we would have a demanding and ethical set of standards by which to judge accomplished university teaching.

The capability approach is multi-dimensional so that development in all its complexity must be taken up, avoiding easy domestication through a focus on single capabilities. The complexity of the approach should be seen not as a difficulty but as an advantage. As Barnett and Hallam (1999) argue, we live in an increasingly complex world – we should not be surprised that higher education shares that complexity and we should not then seek to reduce it to formulaic prescriptions for action which are unhelpful at best. As Colby *et al.* (2003: 7) further note, the complexity of our social, economic and political worlds is 'accelerating at an alarming pace', and Touraine (2000: 13) explains that we inhabit a world of 'permanent and uncontrollable change'. Pedagogy after all is complex and we risk its technicization when we search for simplistic generic formulas for 'what works'; rather than dealing with complexity in our practice and educational research in the twenty-first century. Instead we should be asking, 'works for whom, where, under what conditions, and why?' Moreover, research in the USA on supporting professional learning communities in schools suggests that multiple indicators create sophisticated images of change, which are more convincing than single scales of failure or success (Hargreaves, 2003). Collecting data on student capability would then inform the improvement of practice in local contexts, inform continuous learning about university teaching, and do this ideally in shared communities of inquiry.

That the capability approach offers an alternative language or discourse to talk about teaching and learning in higher education should not be underestimated. The language of neo-liberalism in higher education seeps into our consciousness and shapes our practices and identities. Bronwyn Davies (2005) offers a powerful indictment of such neo-liberal regimes in university life, citing Toni Morrison's explication of the limiting force of oppressive language which 'does more than represent violence; it is violence; does more than represent the limits of knowledge; it limits knowledge' (1993: 16, quoted in Davies, 2005: 6). Davies (2005: 6) argues that this 'powerful relanguaging' of academic work is further tied to our economic survival. She recounts conversations among academics 'who are not otherwise monsters but have become monstrous in their will to survive and their attention to the bottom line'. We are colonized through audit into 'pathologies of creative compliance', John Elliott (2001) explains, we become, or learn to perform, our compliance.

By linking higher education to an expansive discourse of human development, explored from multidisciplinary frameworks as in the capability approach, we might locate pedagogy in a broader framework, international and global in its concerns, crossing boundaries of North and South, rich and poor. It means asking: [educational] development for whom and [educational] development for what as a matter both for regions and countries, but also as a global concern. This wider development discourse foregrounds poverty reduction, and locating higher education within its boundaries says implicitly that quality of life and human well-being, globally, is a matter for us all. This conceptual link to a moral language of human development potentially reconstructs how we speak about higher education pedagogy. It is to underline that in a plural world of difference, higher education should be part of the solution not part of the problem. Our task is to create an awareness 'that the only way in which we can live our lives is with others' (Gert Biesta, quoted in Englund, 2002: 285). We have, says Touraine (2000: 15), 'to conceive and construct new forms of collective and personal life'. Similarly, the Delors UNESCO Commission on Education (1996) outlined four pillars of education – learning to live together, to understand, to do, and to be. Not only does this resonate with the capability approach and its valuable beings and doings, it further emphasizes the importance of inter-cultural communication, respect and understanding. As the Commission (1996: 18) noted, 'We have to learn to live together by developing our understanding of others'. For higher education in contemporary times to set itself apart from this project, not least in its teaching and learning practices with diverse students, should be deeply worrying.

A criterion of justice

Finally, then, I return to the importance of a criterion of justice in our deliberations, practices and evaluations of teaching and learning in higher education. I suggested that the advantages of the capability approach as a framework for a criterion of justice in higher education are: (i) that higher education has intrinsic and instrumental value; (ii) it addresses both recognition and redistribution, (iii) it foregrounds agency as a measure of individual dis/advantage in and through higher education; (iv) it locates individual agency and social and institutional arrangements on the same plane; and (v) it focuses on the capabilities needed to achieve educational/pedagogical rights. The approach further seeks to rework the boundaries between educational action and conceptual critique in its focus on beings and doings. We need to ask not only which capabilities matter, but how well we are doing practically in higher education in fostering these capabilities. Added to this is the explicit attention to distributional issues and concerns with education equality. Not only does the educational development of each student matter, but we need to pay attention also to interpersonal comparison in the space of capabilities in order to address equity and equality. Who gets to develop valued capabilities, and who is constrained in such development are then a matter of both the distribution of resources and of capability for equality and agency achievement in higher education.

In my view, the capability approach offers a vision of what ought to be in teaching and learning in higher education, providing a normative framework to orient educational development in universities. When combined with a discourse of (pedagogic) rights, it further foregrounds both power and the obligations of those involved in educational development (Eyben, 2003). The capability approach, I would argue, is a 'thick' form of thinking about equality and justice on, in and through higher education practice and related education policy, compared to the 'thin' view of teaching and learning in higher education which currently dominates most policy assumptions and much of the practice debate. I argue that the capability approach takes us beyond 'thin' approaches to teaching and learning and beyond sociological analyses of higher education, which offer important critiques but say little about practice. The capability approach is a critical analysis *for* higher education, not only *of* higher education. It offers a language not only to identify moments of equity and the persistence of normalizing and alienating practices, but also a practical framework for acting towards, and for judging equality. It fleshes out Barnett's (1997) key ideas of 'criticality' and 'critical being', foregrounding agency freedom and agency achievement. It is, I suggest, an ethical narrative of and for higher education pedagogy.

Touraine (2000) argues that we become Subjects throughout our lives, so that we need to 'reflect on our past experiences, and to prepare our choices for the future'. It also then follows that not only schools, but colleges and universities also contribute to this process of becoming, and to education as identity formation and re-formation. In a changing society, he says, institutions 'can do less and less to predict their [students'] trajectory'. People move from one country to another, they experience diverse home circumstances, and so on. Touraine argues that educational institutions are 'not here for society's benefit', not there even to train citizens or workers. Their purpose is 'to enhance individuals to become Subjects' of their own personal life-project' (2000: 273), because every one desires 'to be the actor in his or her existence' (2000: 304). For Touraine, education should therefore be 'above all a way of developing the capacity to act and think in the name of a creative personal freedom that cannot be developed without coming into contact with the intellectual, technological and ethical constructs of both the past and the present' (2000: 282). Crucially, what Touraine has in mind in this process of becoming a Subject is not individualistic consumerism. As he points out, what is anyway individual about a consumer whose demands are determined by the media and *laissez-faire* economics? He defends not an individualism that is indifferent to public life, but rather one that supports the capacity of social actors to participate in public affairs. Touraine has in mind a democratic process and democratizing system which respects freedom for all and recognizes that 'the Other enjoys the same freedom' (2000: 284).

The goal of (higher) education is then to train and educate persons 'to be themselves, to enable them to become free individuals who can discover and preserve the unity of their experience throughout the upheavals and despite the pressures that are brought to bear on them' (2000: 284). We need, he argues, to create social conditions 'that can safeguard both personal freedom and cultural diversity' (2000: 299), and 'defend an ideal of solidarity' (2000: 299). The idea of justice, Touraine advocates, 'results in a struggle to place limitations on all forms of power by demanding the recognition of both social rights, which can be defined in terms of justice and fairness, and cultural rights, which can be formulated in terms of identity and difference' (2000: 302). We might express this idea of justice pedagogically in terms of a pedagogy which recognizes that power permeates pedagogy but that inequalities of power and cultural differences between lecturers and students and students and students need (should) not be oppressive if we recognize the fostering of student capabilities as core to any progressive pedagogical project. Touraine's ideas have strong resonances with navigational, resilience, aspirational, dignity and self-reflexive capabilities, and overall capabilities offer a practical way to address Touraine's idea of justice.

What is fundamentally at issue in all this, is an argument for justice as a criterion for a twenty-first-century higher pedagogy. Nussbaum (2002) forcefully underlines the case again when she argues that:

Today's universities are shaping future citizens in an age of cultural diversity and increasing internationalization. All modern democracies are inescapably plural . . . If our institutions of higher education do not build a richer network of human connections it is likely that our dealings with one another will be mediated by the defective norms of market exchange. A rich network of human connections, however, will not arise magically out of our good intentions: we need to think about how our educational institutions contribute to that goal.

(2002: 291–2)

I believe the capability approach applied in higher education, and specifically to guide and evaluate pedagogy, contributes to teaching and learning for 'a richness of human understanding and aspiration that cannot be supplied by economic connections alone' (Nussbaum, 2002: 292). It is to reiterate the argument that higher education provides maps and knowledge for new ways of understanding self and the world for graduates' life patterns and occupations beyond university. At issue is whether higher education encourages students to develop maps for civic and social responsibility and democratic public life, or for consumerism, individualism and private gain, even as we recognize that we cannot and should not predict or prescribe our students' future pathways (Arendt, 1977).

The capability approach addresses both processes and outcomes of learning and pedagogy. It robustly challenges the narrowness of human capital theory in which human lives are viewed as the means to economic gain. It raises the importance of a participatory and deliberative development of higher education practice and policy. It reclaims a language of choice as freedom and autonomy as both independence and a network of ethical obligations. Above all, it points to a problem and suggests a practical approach. It requires not only that we talk about and theorize change but that we are able to point to and *do* change through its focus on beings and doings in and through higher education.

What has been stressed in this book is that pedagogy is a relay for normalizing relations of power, which can be interrupted so that equity and transformation possibilities emerge. It is to refuse pessimism and to acknowledge that 'it is the teachers who have to intervene' (Touraine, 2000: 287). In all this, this book has attempted to show that the capability approach takes our thinking forward in promising and exciting directions, for justice and for educational development in higher education teaching and learning. It is appropriate to close with Touraine's (2000: 265) powerful words. Any educational programme, including higher education, he argues, is 'the clearest manifestation of a society's spirit'.

What spirit, then, are we developing in our universities and higher education systems? Ought we to be doing better in educational policy and institutional conditions to enable capability pedagogies? Even if higher education pedagogy cannot do everything in the face of unfavourable economic and social arrangements (Sen's 'instrumental freedoms'), a higher education pedagogy of capabilities can, in my view, do *something* to question and critique higher education and public life being regulated by markets.

Notes

1 The interview was collected as part of the 'Teaching for Critical Learning' project. The lecturer has been given a pseudonym.

Bibliography

Alkire, S. (2001) Dimensions of Human Development, *World Development*, 30(2): 181–205 (Available on line at http://www.sciencedirect.com/science. Accessed 6 January 2005)

Alkire, S. (2002) *Valuing Freedoms. Sen's Capability Approach and Poverty Reduction.* Oxford: Oxford University Press

Appadurai, A. (2004) The Capacity to Aspire: Culture and the Terms of Recognition; in V. Rao and M. Walton (eds) *Culture and Public Action.* Stanford: Stanford University Press

Appiah, K.A. (2005) *The Ethics of Identity.* Princeton: Princeton University Press

Apple, M. (1993) *Official Knowledge, Democratic Education in a Conservative Age.* New York: Routledge

Apple, M. (2001) Comparing neo-liberal projects and inequality in education, *Comparative Education*, 37(4): 409–23

Archer, L., Hutchings, M. and Ross, A. (2003) *Higher Education and Social Class: Issues of exclusion and inclusion.* London: RoutledgeFalmer

Arendt, H. (1977) *Between Past and Future.* Harmondsworth: Penguin Books

Arneson, R. (2000) Perfectionism and Politics, *Ethics*, 111(1): 37–63 (available on-line at http://philosophy2.ucsd.edu/~rarneson/PERFECTIONISM4.HTM. Accessed 12 December 2004)

Aronowitz, S. and Giroux, H. (2000) The corporate university and the politics of education, *The Educational Forum*, 64: 332–9

Ashwin, P. and McLean, M. (2004) Towards an integration of the 'Approaches to Learning' and 'Critical Pedagogy' perspectives in higher education through a focus on academic engagement. Paper presented to the British Educational Research Association special interest group on higher education, University of Oxford, May 2004

Aung San Suu Kyi (1995) Freedom, Development and Human Worth, *Journal of Democracy*, 6(2): 11–19

Bagnall, R.G. (2002) The Contingent University: an ethical critique, *Educational Philosophy and Theory*, 34(1): 77–90

Ball, S., Maguire, M. and Macrae, S. (2000a) *Choices, Pathways and Transitions Post-16.* London: RoutledgeFalmer

Ball, S., David, M., Davies, J. and Reay, D. (2000b) Ranking, Reputation and Reflexivity:

Student Choice of Higher Education in the UK. Paper presented at the annual conference of the British Educational Research Association, Cardiff, September 2000

Ball, S., Davies, J., David, M. and Reay, D. (2002) 'Classification' and 'judgement': social class and the 'cognitive structures' of choice in higher education, *British Journal of Sociology of Education*, 23(1): 51–72

Barclay, L. (2003) What kind of liberal is Martha Nussbaum?, *Nordic Journal of Philosophy*, 4(2): 5–24

Barnett, R. (ed.) (1992) *Learning to effect*. Buckingham: SRHE/Open University Press

Barnett, R. (1997) *Higher Education: A Critical Business*. Buckingham: SRHE/Open University Press

Barnett, R. (2000) *Realizing the University in an Age of Supercomplexity*. Buckingham: SRHE/Open University Press.

Barnett, R. (2003) *Beyond All Reason. Living with Ideology in the University*. Maidenhead: SRHE/Open University Press

Barnett, R. and Coate, K. (2005) *Engaging the Curriculum in Higher Education*. Maidenhead: SRHE/Open University Press

Barnett, R. and Hallam, S. (1999) Teaching for Supercomplexity: A Pedagogy for Higher Education; in P. Mortimore (ed.) *Understanding Pedagogy And Its Impact on Learning*. London: Paul Chapman Publishing

Barr, J. (2002) Universities after postmodernism, *International Journal of Lifelong Education*, 21(4): 321–33

Bates, R. (2004) Developing Capabilities and the Management of Trust: Where Administration Went Wrong. Paper presented to the Australian Association for Research in Education annual conference, Melbourne, December 2004

Bates, R. (2005) Can We Live Together? Towards a global curriculum, *Arts and Humanities in Higher Education*, 4(1): 95–110

Bathmaker A.M. and Avis, J. (2005) Is that 'tingling feeling' enough? Constructions of teaching and learning in further education, *Educational Review*, 57(1): 3–20

Bauman, Z. (2001) *Community*. Cambridge: Polity Press

Becher, T. and Trowler, P. (2001) *Academic Tribes and Territories: Intellectual Inquiry and the Cultures of Disciplines*. Buckingham: SRHE/Open University Press

Beck, U. (1992) *Risk and Society*. London: Sage

Belenky, M.F., Clinchy, B.M., Goldberger, N.R. and Tarule, J.M. (1986) *Women's Ways of Knowing: the Development of Self, Voice and Mind*. New York: Basic Books

Berge, B-M. and Ve, H. (2000) *Action Research for Gender Equity*. Buckingham: Open University Press

Bernstein, B. (2000) *Pedagogy, Symbolic Control and Identity*. London: Routledge

Biesta, G., Hodkinson, P. and Goodson, I. (2004) Combining Life History and Life-Course Approaches in Researching Lifelong Learning. Paper presented at the annual conference of the Teaching and Learning Research programme, November 2004

Biggeri, M., Libanora, R., Mariani, S., and Menchini, L. (2004) Children Establishing Their Capabilities: Preliminary Results of the Survey During the First Children's World Congress on Child Labour. Paper presented at the Fourth International Conference on the Capability Approach, 5–7 September 2004, University of Pavia, Italy.

Biggs, J. (2003) *Teaching for Quality Learning at University*, 2nd ed. Buckingham: SRHE/Open University Press

Blake, N., Smith, R. and Standish, P. (1998) *The Universities We Need. Higher Education after Dearing.* London: Kogan Page

Bloomer, M. and Hodkinson, P. (2000) Learning careers: continuity and change in young people's dispositions to learning, *British Educational Research Journal,* 26(5): 583–98

Boler, M. (1999) *Feeling Power: Emotions and Education.* New York: Routledge

Bourdieu, P. (1977) *Outline of a Theory of Practice.* Cambridge: Cambridge University Press

Bourdieu, P. (2003) Against objectivism: the reality of the social fiction; in P. Sikes, J. Nixon and W. Carr (eds) *The Moral Foundations of Educational Research: Knowledge, Inquiry and Values.* Maidenhead: Open University Press

Bourdieu, P. and Passeron, J-C. (1977) *Reproduction in Education, Society and Culture,* 2nd ed. London: Sage

Bowl, M. (2003) *Non-Traditional Entrants to Higher Education.* Stoke-on-Trent: Trentham Books

Boyer, E.L. (1987) *College: The undergraduate experience in America.* New York: Harper Collins

Boyer, E.L. (1990) *Scholarship reconsidered: Priorities for the professoriate.* Menlo Park, CA: The Carnegie Foundation for the Advancement of Teaching

Bozalek, V. (2004) Recognition, Resources and Responsibilities: Using Students' Stories of Family to Renew the South African Social Work Curriculum. Unpublished doctoral thesis, Utrecht University

Brabazon, T. (2002) *Digital hemlock. Internet Education and the Poisoning of Teaching.* Sydney: University of New South Wales Press

Bradley, H. (1996) *Fractured Identities: changing patterns of inequality.* Cambridge: Polity Press

Bridges, D. (2000) Back to the Future: the higher education curriculum in the twenty-first century, *Cambridge Journal of Education,* 30(1): 37–56

Bridges, D. (2004) Widening participation in higher education: the philosopher and the bricklayer. Paper presented at the annual conference of the British Educational Research Association, Manchester, September 2004

Brighouse, H. (2000) *School Choice and Social Justice.* Oxford: Oxford University Press

Brighouse, H. (forthcoming) Do children have objective educational interests?

Brighouse, H. and Swift, A (2003) Defending liberalism in education theory, *Journal of Education Policy,* 18(4): 355–73

Brine, J. and Waller, R. (2004) Working class women on an Access course: risk, opportunity and (re)constructing identities, *Gender and Education,* 16(1): 97–114

Brockbank, A. and McGill, I. (1998) *Facilitating Reflective Learning in Higher Education.* Buckingham: SRHE/Open University Press

Carlson, D. (1995) Making Progress: Progressive Education in the Postmodern, *Educational Theory,* 45(3): 337–57

Coate, K. (1999) Feminist Knowledge and the Ivory Tower: a case study, *Gender and Education,* 11(2): 141–61

Colby, A., Ehrlich, T., Beaumont, E., and Stephens, J. (2003) *Educating Citizens. Preparing America's Undergraduates For Lives of Moral And Civic Responsibility.* Menlo Park, CA: The Carnegie Foundation for the Advancement of Teaching

Colley, H. (2003) *Mentoring for Social Inclusion. A critical approach to nurturing mentoring relationships.* London: RoutledgeFalmer

Comim, F. (2003). Capability Dynamics: the importance of time to capability assessments. Paper presented at the Third International Conference on the Capability Approach Conference, August 2003, University of Pavia, Italy

Comim, F. (2004) Measuring capabilities. Presentation to the Capability and Education Network, St Edmunds College, Cambridge, 4 November 2004

Connor, H. (2001) Deciding For or Against Participation in Higher Education: the Views of Young People from Lower Social Class Backgrounds, *Higher Education Quarterly*, 55(2): 204–24

Cribb, A. and Gewirtz, S. (2003) Towards a sociology of just practices: an analysis of plural conceptions of justice; in C. Vincent (ed.) *Social Justice, Education and Identity*. London: RoutledgeFalmer

Dall'Alba, G. and Barnacle, R. (2004) Embodied knowing in higher education. Paper presented to the Australian Association for Research in Education annual conference, Melbourne, December 2004

Davies, B. (2005) The (Im)possibility of Intellectual Work in Neoliberal Regimes, *Discourse*, 26(1): 1–14

Davis, B. (2004) *Inventions of Teaching. A Genealogy*. NJ: Lawrence Erlbaum

Dearing, R. (1997) *Higher Education in the Learning Society (The Dearing Report)*. London: National Committee of Inquiry into Higher Education

Deneulin, S. (2004) Human freedom in the capability approach: capabilities, possibilities and incapabilities. Paper presented at a meeting of the Capability and Education network, St Edmunds College, Cambridge, 18 March 2004

Deneulin, S. (2005) Promoting Human Freedoms under Conditions of Inequalities: a procedural framework, *Journal of Human Development*, 6(1): 75–92

Department for Education and Skills (2003) *The future of higher education*, cm 5735. Norwich: HMSO

Deprez, L. and Butler, S. (2001) The Capabilities Approach and Economic Security for Low Income Women in the US: Securing Access to Higher Education under Welfare Reform. Paper presented at the First International Conference on the Capabilities Approach: Justice and Poverty, Examining Sen's Capability Approach, St Edmunds College, Cambridge September 2001

Dreze, J. and Sen, A. (1995) *India: Economic Development and Social Opportunity*. Oxford: Oxford University Press

Dunne, J. and Pendlebury, S. (2003) Practical Reason; in N. Blake, P. Smeyers, R. Smith and P. Standish (eds) *The Blackwell Guide to the Philosophy of Education*. Oxford: Blackwell

Eco, U. (2004) It's not what you know . . ., *The Guardian*, 3 April 2004: 7

Edwards, R., Ranson, S. and Strain, M. (2002) Reflexivity: towards a theory of lifelong learning, *International Journal of Lifelong Education*, 21(6): 525–36

Eggers, D. (2004) Serve or Fail, *The New York Times*, 13 June 2004

Elliot, J. (2001) Characteristics of performative cultures: their central paradoxes and limitations as resources of educational reform; in D. Gleeson and C. Husbands (eds) *The Performing School*. London: RoutledgeFalmer

Ellsworth, E. (1989) Why Doesn't This Feel Empowering? *Harvard Educational Review*

Elton, L. (2001) Research and teaching: conditions for a positive link, *Teaching in Higher Education*, 6(1): 43–56

Elton, L. and Partington, P. (1993) *Teaching Standards and Excellence in Higher Education*, 2nd ed. Sheffield: CVCP

Englund, T. (2002) Higher Education, Democracy And Citizenship – The Democratic Potential Of The University, *Studies in Philosophy and Education*, 21: 281–7

Entwistle, N. and Ramsden, P. (1983) *Understanding Student Learning*. London: Croom Helm

Evans, M. (2004) *Killing Thinking. The Death of the Universities*. London: Continuum

Eyben, R. (2003) The rise of rights: rights-based approaches to international development, *IDS Policy Briefing* 17

Field, J. (2000) *Lifelong learning and the new educational order*. Stoke-on-Trent: Trentham Books

Flores-Crespo, P. (2001) Sen's human capabilities approach and higher education in Mexico. The case of the Technological University of Tula. Paper presented at the First International Conference on the Capabilities Approach: Justice and Poverty, Examining Sen's Capability Approach, St Edmunds College, Cambridge, September 2001

Flores-Crespo, P. (2004) Situating education in the human capabilities approach, Fourth International Conference on the Capability Approach, University of Pavia, September 2004

Forbes, A. and Wickens, E. (2005) A good social life helps students to stay the course, *The Times Higher Education Supplement*, 28 January 2005: 58

Fraser, N. (1997) *Justice Interruptus. Critical Reflections on the 'Post Socialist' Condition*. London: Routledge

Fraser, N. (1998) Social Justice in the Age of Identity Politics: Redistribution, Recognition and Participation; in G. Petersen (ed.) *The Tanner Lectures on Human Values XIX*. Salt Lake City: University of Utah Press

Freire, P. (1972) *Pedagogy of the Oppressed*. London: Sheed and Ward

Freire, P. (1978) *Education for Critical Consciousness*. New York: Seabury

Freire, P. (1985) *The Politics of Education: Culture, Power, and Liberation*. South Hadley, MA: Bergin and Garvey

Gaita, R. (2000) Truth and the university; in. T. Coady (ed.) *Why Universities Matter*. St Leonards: Allen and Unwin

Gallacher, J., Crossan, B., Field, J. and Merrill, B. (2002) Learning careers and the social space; exploring the fragile identities of adult returners in the new further education, *International Journal of Lifelong Education*, 21(6): 493–509

Gaspar, D. (2004) Subjective and objective well being in relation to economic inputs: puzzles and responses. Paper presented at workshop on Capability and Happiness, St Edmunds College, Cambridge, March 2004.

Gaspar, D. and Van Staveren, I. (2003) Development As Freedom – And As What Else?, *Feminist Economics*, 9(2–3): 137–61

Geertz, C. (2000) *Available Light. Anthropological Reflections on Philosophical Topics*. Princeton, NJ: Princeton University Press

George, E. (2004) Human Rights, Development and the Politics of Gender Based Violence in Schools: Enhancing Girls' Education and the Capabilities Approach. Paper presented at the Fourth International Conference on the Capability Approach, University of Pavia, September 2004

Gewirtz, S. (1998) Conceptualising social justice in education: mapping the field, *Journal of Education Policy*, 13: 469–84

Gibbons, M. *et al.* (1994) *The New Production of Knowledge: The Dynamics of Science and Research in Contemporary Societies*. London: Sage

Giddens, A. (1991) *Modernity and Self-Identity: self and society in the late modern age*. Cambridge: Polity

Giroux, H. (1992) *Border Crossings: Cultural Workers and the Politics of Education*. New York: Routledge

Giroux, H. (2001) Commodification of Higher Education; in H. Giroux and K. Myrsiades (eds) (2001) *Beyond the Corporate University*. Lanham: Rowman and Littlefield

Giroux, H. and Myrsiades, K. (eds) (2001) *Beyond the Corporate University*. Lanham: Rowman and Littlefield Publishers

Goddard, A. (2003) Here's what we think university is for Mr Clarke 1, *Times Higher Education Supplement*, 23 May 2003 (available online at http://www.thes.co.uk/search/story.aspx. Accessed 11 April 2005)

Gore, J. (1993) *The Struggle for Pedagogies: Critical and feminist discourses as regimes of truth*. New York: Routledge

Greene, M. and Griffiths, M. (2003) Feminism, Philosophy and Education: Imagining Public Spaces; in N. Blake, P. Smeyers, R. Smith and P. Standish (eds) *The Blackwell Guide to the Philosophy of Education*. Oxford: Blackwell

Griffiths, M. (1998) *Educational Research for Social Justice: getting off the fence*. Buckingham: Open University Press

Hage, G. (2001) The Shrinking Society: Ethics and Hope in the Era of Global Capitalism (available online at http://subsol.c3.hu/subsol_2/contributors2/hagetext.html. Accessed 6 December 2004)

Haggis, T. (2003) Constructing Images of Ourselves? A Critical Investigation into 'Approaches to Learning' Research in Higher Education, *British Educational Research Journal*, 29(1): 89–104

Halsey, A.H. (1992) *Decline of Donnish Dominion*. Oxford: Clarendon Press

Hargreaves, A. (2003) *Teaching in the Knowledge Society. Education in an age of insecurity*. Maidenhead and Philadelphia: Open University Press

Harland, T. (2002) Zoology Students' Experiences of Collaborative Enquiry in Problem-Based Learning, *Teaching in Higher Education*, 7(1): 3–16

Harvard University (2004) *A Report on the Harvard College Curricular Review*, April 2004. Faculty of Arts and Sciences, Harvard University (available on-line at http://www.harvard.edu. Accessed 30 April, 2005).

Heidegger, M. (1968) *What is called thinking?* Trans. J.G. Gray. New York: Harper Row

Higgins, J. (2001) Critical thinking on the path to peace, *Times Higher Education Supplement*, 19 March 2001: 22

Higher Education Capability Forum (1988) *The Capability Manifesto* (available online at http://www.lle.mdx.ac.uk/hec/manifesto.htm. Accessed 20 June 2004)

Hodges, L. (2005) A World of Difference, *The Independent*, 13 January 2005: 6

Honneth, A. (1995) *The Struggle for Recognition: The Moral Grammar of Social Conflicts*. Cambridge: Polity Press

hooks, b. (1994) *Teaching to Transgress. Education as the Practice of Freedom*. New York: Routledge

Hughes, C. (2002) *Key Concepts in Feminist Theory and Research*. London: Sage

Hughes, C. (2004) New Times? New Learners? New Voices? Towards a contemporary social theory of learning, *British Journal of Sociology of Education*, 25(3): 395–408

Hurston, Z.N. (1942) *Dust Tracks on a Road*. Philadelphia: J.B. Pippincott and Company

Huttunen, R. and Heikkinen, L.T.H. (2004) Teaching and the Dialectic of Recognition, *Pedagogy, Culture and Society*, 12(2): 163–73

Inglis, F. (2004) Education and the Good Society (2); in F. Inglis (ed.) *Education and the Good Society*. Houndmills: Palgrave Macmillan

Jackson, S. (2003) Lifelong Earning: working class women and lifelong learning, *Gender and Education*, 15(4): 365–76

Jenkins A. (2000) The relationship between teaching and research: where does geography stand and deliver?, *Journal of Geography in Higher Education*, 24(3): 325–51

Jonathan, R. (2001) Higher Education Transformation and the Public Good, *Kagisano Higher Education Discussion Series*, 1: 28–63

Kerr, D. (2002) Devoid of community: Examining conceptions of autonomy in education, *Educational Theory*, 52(1): 1–16 (available on line at http://proquest. umi.com/ Accessed 10 December 2004)

Kincheloe, J. (2004) *Critical Pedagogy*. New York: Peter Lang

Krog, A. (1999) *Country of My Skull*. London: Vintage

Kuhn, A. (1995) *Family Secrets*. London: Verso

Lakeman, L. (1989) Women, Violence and the Montreal Massacre (available online at http://www.rapereliefshelter.bc.ca/dec6/leearticle.html. Accessed 25 January 2005)

Lankshear, C. and McLaren. P. (1993) *Critical Literacy: Politics, Praxis and the Postmodern*. Albany: SUNY Press

Lather, P. (1991) *Getting Smart: Feminist research and pedagogy with/in the postmodern*. New York: Routledge

Lea, M.R. and Street, B.V. (1998) Student writing in higher education: an academic literacies approach, *Studies in Higher Education*, 23: 157–72

Leistyna, P. and Woodrum, A. (1996) Context and Culture: What Is Critical Pedagogy?; in Leistyna, P., Woodrum, A., and Sherblom, S. (eds) (1996) *Breaking Free. The Transformative Power of Critical Pedagogy*. Cambridge, MA: Harvard Educational Review

Leistyna, P., Woodrum, A., and Sherblom, S. (eds) (1996) *Breaking Free. The Transformative Power of Critical Pedagogy*. Cambridge, MA: Harvard Educational Review

Lewis, M.G. (1993) *Without a word: teaching beyond women's silence*. New York and London: Routledge

Light, R. J. (2001) *Making the Most of College. Students Speak Their Minds*. Cambridge, MA: Harvard University Press

Lingard, B. (2005). Socially Just Pedagogies in Changing Times. Paper presented at the Philosophy of Education seminar, University of Sheffield, 10 March 2005

Little, A. (2003) Motivating Learning and the Development of Human Capital, *Compare*, 33(4): 437–52

Lucas, L. (2004) Reclaiming Academic Research Work from Regulation and Relegation; in M. Walker and J. Nixon (eds) (2004) *Reclaiming Universities from a Runaway World*. Maidenhead: SRHE/Open University Press

Luke, C. and Gore, J. (eds.) (1992) *Feminisms and Critical Pedagogy*. New York: Routledge

McLaren, P. (1989) *Life in Schools: An Introduction to Critical Pedagogy in the Foundations of Education*. New York: Longman

McLaren, P. (1995) *Critical Pedagogy and Predatory Culture: Oppositional Politics in a Postmodern Era*. New York: Routledge

McLeod, J. (2003) Revisiting gender, habitus, and social capital, or why Bourdieu now? Paper presented at the 3rd international conference on Gender and Education, Sheffield, April 2003

McNay, L. (2000) *Gender and Agency*. Cambridge: Polity Press

Mann, S. (2001) Alternative Perspectives on the Student Experience: alienation and engagement, *Studies in Higher Education*, 26(1): 7–19

Marshall, D. and Case, J. (2005) 'Approaches to learning' research in higher education: a response to Haggis, *British Journal of Educational Research*, 31(2): 257–68

Martin, J. (2000) *Coming of Age in Academe*. New York and London: Routledge

Marton, F. and Booth, M. (1997) *Learning and Awareness*. Hillsdale, NJ: Lawrence Erlbaum

Misra, M. (2005) Sparring is one of the healthiest pursuits, *The Times Higher Education Supplement*, 4 March 2005: 58

Morley, L. (1997) A Class of One's Own; in P. Mahony and C. Zmroczek (eds) *Class Matters. 'Working-Class' Women's Perspectives on Social Class*. London: Taylor and Francis

Morley, L. (1999) *Organising feminisms: the micropolitics of the academy*. London: Macmillan

Morley, L. (2003) *Quality and Power in Higher Education*. Maidenhead: SRHE/Open University Press

Morrison, T. (1993) *Lecture and speech of acceptance, upon the award of the Nobel prize for literature, delivered in Stockholm on the seventh of December, nineteen hundred and ninety-three*. London: Chatto and Windus

Mpumlwana, N. (2000) The Monster of Professional Power, *Teaching in Higher Education*, 5(4): 535–40

Naidoo, R. (2003) Repositioning Higher Education as a Global Commodity: opportunities and challenges for future sociology of education work, *British Journal of Sociology of Education*, 24(2): 249–59

Narayan, D. and Petesch, P. (2002) *Voices of the Poor From Many Lands*. Washington: The World Bank

Nixon, J. (2005) Origins and beginnings, as though a vision were revealed to her; in M. Griffiths, *Action for Social Justice in Education. Fairly Different*. Maidenhead: Open University Press

Nixon, J., Martin, J., McKeown, P. and Ranson, S. (1997) Confronting 'failure': towards a pedagogy of recognition, *International Journal of Inclusive Education*, 1(2): 121–41

Nnaemeka, O. (2003) Nego-Feminism: Theorizing, Practicing and Pruning Africa's Way, *Signs*, 29(2): 357–85

Noble, D. (1992) *A World Without Women*. New York and Oxford: Oxford University Press

Nussbaum, M. (1990) *Love's Knowledge. Essays on Philosophy and Literature*. Oxford: Oxford University Press

Nussbaum, M. (1993) Non-Relative Virtues: An Aristotelian Approach; in M. Nussbaum and A. Sen (eds) (1993) *The Quality of Life*. Oxford: Clarendon Press

Nussbaum, M. (1997) *Cultivating Humanity. A Classical Defence of Reform in Liberal Education*. Cambridge, MA: Harvard University Press

Nussbaum, M. (1998) The Good as Discipline, the Good as Freedom; in D.A. Crocker and T. Linden (eds) *Ethics of Consumption*. Lanham: Rowman and Littlefield Publishers

Nussbaum, M. (2000a) *Women and Human Development*. Cambridge: Cambridge University Press

Nussbaum, M. (2000b) Aristotle, Politics and Human Capabilities: A response to Anthony, Arneson, Charlesworth, and Mulgan, *Ethics*, 111(1): 102–40

Nussbaum, M. (2001) *Upheavals Of Thought*. Cambridge: Cambridge University Press

Nussbaum, M. (2002) Education For Citizenship In An Era Of Global Connection, *Studies in Philosophy and Education*, 21: 289–303

Nussbaum, M. (2003a) Capabilities As Fundamental Entitlements: Sen And Social Justice, *Feminist Economics*, 9(2–3): 33–59

Nussbaum, M. (2003b) Political Liberalism and Respect: A Response to Linda Barclay, *Nordic Journal of Philosophy*, 4(2): 25–44

Nussbaum, M. (2004) Liberal Education and Global Community, *Liberal Education*, Winter 2004 (available online at http://www.aacu-edu.org/liberaleducation/le-wi04feature4.cfm. Accessed 25 January 2005)

Nussbaum, M. and Sen, A. (eds) (1993) *The Quality of Life*. Oxford: Clarendon Press

O'Byrne, C. (2004) Valuable beings and doings at third level: a capabilities perspective on higher education. Unpublished doctoral paper, University of Sheffield.

O'Connor, C. (2002) Black Women Beating the Odds from One Generation to the Next: How the Changing Dynamics of Constraint and Opportunity Affect the Process of Educational Resilience, *American Educational Research Journal*, 39(4): 855–903

Okin, S. M. (2003) Poverty, Well-Being, and Gender: What Counts, Who's Heard?, *Philosophy and Public Affairs*, 31: 280–316

Okri, B. (2003) Our work is to free talent in the project of humanity, *Times Higher Educational Supplement*, 20 June 2003: 20

O'Neill, O. (1996) *Towards Justice and Virtue*. Cambridge: Cambridge University Press

Osborn, M., Broadfoot, P., McNess, E., Planel, C., Ravn, B. and Triggs, P. with Cousin, O. and Winther-Jensen, T. (2003) *A world of difference? Comparing learners across Europe*. Maidenhead: Open University Press

Page, E. (2004) Teacher and pupil development and capabilities. Work in progress, presented at the Capability and Education Network seminar, St Edmunds College, Cambridge, 1 June 2004

Papestephanou, M. (2002) Arrows Not Yet Fired: Cultivating Cosmopolitanism Through Education, *Journal of Philosophy of Education*, 36(1): 69–86

Paterson, L. (2000) Higher Education and European Regionalism. Paper presented at the European Conference on Educational Research, Edinburgh, September 2000

Peters, M. (2004) Higher Education, Globalization and the Knowledge Economy; in M. Walker and J. Nixon (eds) (2004) *Reclaiming Universities from a Runaway World*. Maidenhead: SRHE/Open University Press

Pettit, J. and Wheeler, S. (2005) Developing Rights? Relating Discourse to Context and Practice, *IDS Bulletin Developing Rights*, 36(1): 1–8

Phipps, A. and Gonzalez, M. (2004) *Modern Languages. Learning and Teaching in an Intercultural Field*. London: Sage Publications

Plummer, G. (2000) *Failing working-class girls*. Stoke-on-Trent: Trentham Press

Pollard, A. (2003) Learning through life: higher education and the lifecourse of individuals; in M. Slowey and D. Watson (eds) *Higher Education and the Lifecourse*. Maidenhead: SRHE/Open University Press

Power, S. and Gerwirtz, S. (2001) Reading Education Action Zones, *Journal of Education Policy*, 16(1): 39–51

Prosser, M. and Trigwell, K. (1998) *Teaching for Learning in Higher Education*. Buckingham: SRHE/Open University Press

Pyle, A. (1999) Key Philosophers in Conversation. The Cogito Interviews. London: Routledge

Quinn, J. (2003) *Powerful Subjects*. Stoke-on-Trent: Trentham Books

Ranson, S. (1998) *Inside the Learning Society*. London: Cassell

Rao, V. and Walton, M. (2004) Culture and Public Action: Relationality, Equality of Agency and Development; in V. Rao and M. Walton (eds) *Culture and Public Action*. Stanford: Stanford University Press

Rawls, J. (2001) *Justice as Fairness. A Restatement*. Cambridge, MA: The Belknap Press

Raynor, J. (2004) Girls' development and capabilities in Bangladesh. Work in progress, presented at the Capability and Education Network seminar, St Edmunds College, Cambridge, 1 June 2004

Readings, B. (1996) *The University in Ruins*. Cambridge, MA: Harvard University Press

Reay, D. (2004) Finding or losing yourself? Working class relationships to education; in S. Ball (ed.) *The RoutledgeFalmer Reader in Sociology of Education*. London: RoutledgeFalmer

Record, J. (2003) UNH Speaker: Women's literacy a global challenge (available online at http://www.law.uchicago.edu/news/nussbaum-unh.html. Accessed 10 February 2005)

Rhodes, F.H.T. (1993) The Place of Teaching in the Research University; in J.R. Cole, E.G. Barber and S.R. Graubard (eds) *The Research University in a Time of Discontent*. Baltimore: The Johns Hopkins University Press

Ricoeur, R. (1991) *Lectures autour du Politique*. Paris: Seuil

Rigsby, D.W. (1994) On Resilience: Questions of Validity; in M. Wang and E. Gordon (eds) *Educational resilience in inner-city America*. Mahwah, NJ: Lawrence Erlbaum

Rizvi, F. (2005) International education and the production of cosmopolitan identities, *RIHE International Publications Series*, 9 (available online at http://www.Cgs.uiuc.edu/resources/conf_seminars_workshops/TSRizvi.pdf. Accessed 15 March 2005)

Robeyns, I (2003a) Is Nancy Fraser's Critique of Theories of Distributive Justice Justified?, *Constellations* 10(4): 538–53

Robeyns, I. (2003b) Sen's Capability Approach and Gender Inequality: Selecting Relevant Capabilities, *Feminist Economics*, 9(2–3): 61–91

Robeyns, I. (2004) Justice as Fairness and the Capability Approach. Paper presented at the Fourth International Conference on the Capability Approach, University of Pavia, September 2004

Robeyns, I. (2005) The Capability Approach – A Theoretical Survey, *Journal of Human Development*, 6(1): 93–114

Ropers-Huilman, B. (1998) *Feminist Teaching in Theory and Practice*. New York: Teachers College Press

Rothenberg, P. (2000) *Invisible privilege. A memoir about race, class and gender*. Kansas: University Press of Kansas

Rowland, S. (1996) Relationships between teaching and research, *Teaching in Higher Education*, 1(1): 7–20

Rowland, S. (2000) *The Enquiring University Teacher*. Buckingham: SRHE/Open University Press

Rowland, S. (2001) Is the University a Place of Learning? Compliance and contestation in higher education. Inaugural professorial lecture, University College, London, November 2001

Rubin, L. (1976) *Worlds of Pain: Life in the Working Class Family*. New York: Basic Books

Ruth, D. (1993) First Fruits, What it is like to come to UWC; in M. Walker (ed.) *AD Dialogues 1 Explorations in Change*. Bellville: University of the Western Cape

Ryan, A. (2001) *Feminist Ways of Knowing*. Leicester: National Institute of Adult and Continuing Education

Said, E. (1994) *Representations of the Intellectual. The 1993 Reith lectures*. London: Vintage

Saito, M. (2003) Amartya Sen's Capability Approach to Education: A Critical Exploration, *Journal of Philosophy of Education*, 37(1): 17–34

Schuller, T., Brasett-Grundy, A., Green, A., Hammond, C. and Preston, J. (2002)
Learning, Continuity and Change in Adult Life. London: Institute of Education

Scott, M. (2004) Student, critic and literary text; a discussion of 'critical thinking'; in
M. Tight (ed.) *The RoutledgeFalmer Reader in Higher Education*. London:
RoutledgeFalmer

Seddon, T. (2003) Framing justice: challenges for research, *Journal of Education Policy*,
18(3): 229–52

Seldon, S. (2004) The Neo-Conservative Assault on the Undergraduate Curriculum;
in M. Walker and J. Nixon (eds) (2004) *Reclaiming Universities from a Runaway
World*. Maidenhead: SRHE/Open University Press

Sen, A. (1985) *Commodities and Capabilities*. Amsterdam: New Holland

Sen, A. (1992) *Inequality Re-examined*. Oxford: Oxford University Press

Sen, A. (1993) Capability and Well Being; in M. Nussbaum and A. Sen (eds) *The
Quality of Life*. Oxford: Oxford University Press

Sen, A. (1999) *Development as Freedom*. New York: Knopf

Sen, A. (2002) *Rationality and Freedom*. Cambridge MA: Belknap Press

Sen, A. with Agarwal, B., Humphries, J., and Robeyns, I.(2003) Continuing the
Conversation, *Feminist Economics*, 9(2–3): 319–32

Sen, A. (2004) Capabilities, Lists and Public Reason: Continuing the Conversation,
Feminist Economics, 10(3): 77–80

Sennett, R. (2003) *Respect. The Formation of Character in an Age of Inequality*. London:
Allen Lane

Sennett, R. and Cobb, J. (1972) *The Hidden Injuries of Class*. Cambridge: Cambridge
University Press

Shore, K. (2003) Gender Researcher Seeks Answers on South African Campuses
(Available online at hhttp://web.idrc.ca/en/ev–33995–201–1-DO_TOPIC>html.
Accessed 25 January 2005)

Singh, M. (2003) Universities and Society: whose terms of engagement?; in
S. Bjarnason and P. Coldstream (eds) *The Idea of Engagement: Universities in Society*.
London: Association of Commonwealth Universities

Skeggs, B. (1997) Classifying Practices; in P. Mahony and C. Zmroczek (eds) *Class
Matters. 'Working-Class' Women's Perspectives on Social Class*. London: Taylor and
Francis

Spelman, E. (2000) How do they see you?, *London Review of Books*, 16 November 2000

Stanton-Salazar, R.D. (1997) A Social Capital Framework for Understanding the
Socialization of Racial Minority Children and Youths, *Harvard Educational Review*,
67(1): 1–36

Stephenson, J. and Weil, S. (1992) *Quality in Learning: a Capability Approach in Higher
Education*. London: Kogan Page

Stewart, F. (2004) Groups and capabilities. Plenary paper presented at the Fourth
International Conference on the Capability Approach, University of Pavia,
September 2004

Stromquist, N. (2002) *Education in a Globalized World. The Connectivity of Economic
Power, Technology and Knowledge*. Lanham: Rowman and Littlefield Publishers

Taylor, C. (1992) Multiculturalism and the politics of recognition; in A. Gutmann
(ed.) *Multiculturalism*. Princeton, NJ: Princeton University Press

Taylor, R., Barr, J. and Steele, T. (2002) *For a Radical Higher Education*. Buckingham:
SRHE/Open University Press

Terzi, L. (2003) A Capability Perspective on Impairment, Disability and Special Needs: Towards Social Justice in Education. Paper presented at the Third International Conference on the Capability Approach, University of Pavia, September 2003

Terzi, L. (2004) On Education as Basic Capability. Paper presented at the Fourth International Conference on the Capability Approach, University of Pavia, September 2004

Tett, L. (2000) I'm Working Class and Proud of It' – gendered experiences of non-traditional participants in higher education, *British Journal of Sociology of Education*, 21(4): 183–94

Thomas, L. (2002) Student retention in higher education: the role of institutional habitus, *Journal of Education Policy*, 17(4): 423–42

Tight, M. (1996) *Key Concepts in Adult Education and Training*. London: Routledge

Tompkins, J. (1996) *A Life In School. What the Teacher Learned*. Reading, Mass: Perseus Books

Touraine, A. (2000) *Can We Live Together? Equality and Difference*. Cambridge: Polity Press

Toynbee, P. (2004) A hedonist's charter, *The Guardian*, 9 April 2004: 23

UNESCO (1996) *Commission on Education*, ed. Jacques Delors. Paris: UNESCO

Unterhalter, E. (2001) The capabilities approach and gendered education: An examination of South African complexities. Paper presented at the First International Conference on the Capabilities Approach: Justice and Poverty, Examining Sen's Capability Approach, St Edmunds College, Cambridge, September 2001

Unterhalter, E. (2003a) Crossing Disciplinary Boundaries: the potential of Sen's capability approach for sociologists of education, *British Journal of Sociology of Education*, 24(5): 665–70

Unterhalter, E. (2003b) The capabilities approach and gendered education, *Theory and Research in Education*, 1(1): 7–22

Unterhalter, E. (2004a) Gender Equality and Education in South Africa: Measurements, scores and strategies. Paper presented to the conference on Gender and Education, Cape Town, May 2004

Unterhalter, E. (2004b) Gender, schooling and global social justice. Paper presented at the Fourth International Conference on the Capability Approach, University of Pavia, September 2004

Unterhalter, E. and Brighouse, H. (2003) Distribution of What? How will we know if we have achieved Education for All by 2015? Paper presented the Third International Conference on the Capabilities Approach: From Sustainable Development to Sustainable Freedom, University of Pavia, September 2003

Utley, A. (2003) Here's what we think university is for Mr Clarke 2, *Times Higher Education Supplement*, 23 May 2003 (available online at http://www.thes. co.uk/search/story.aspx?story_id=92365. Accessed 11 April 2005)

Vaughan, R. (2004) Gender equality and capabilities in education. Paper presented to the Capability and Education Network, St Edmunds College, Cambridge, 4 November 2004

Vincent, C. (2003) *Social Justice, Education and Identity*. London: RoutledgeFalmer

Walker, M. (ed.) (2001a) *Reconstructing Professionalism in University Teaching*. Buckingham: SRHE/Open University Press

Walker, M. (2001b) First generation Students: A pilot study. Unpublished paper, Faculty of Education, University of the West of England

Walker, M. (2002a) Gender justice, knowledge and research: a perspective from education on Nussbaum's capabilities approach. Paper presented at the Second International Conference on the Capability Approach – Promoting Women's Capabilities, Examining Nussbaum's Capabilities Approach, Van Hugel Institute, University of Cambridge, September 2002

Walker, M. (2002b) Pedagogy and the Politics and Purposes of higher Education, *Arts and Humanities in Higher Education*, 1(1): 43–58

Walker, M. (2003) Framing Social Justice In Education: What Does The 'Capabilities' Approach Offer?, *British Journal of Educational Studies*, 51(2): 168–87

Walker, M. (2004a) The capability approach and girls' narratives of life and schooling in South Africa. Paper presented at the Fourth International Conference on the Capability Approach, University of Pavia, September 2004

Walker, M. (2004b) What insight does the capability approach offer to education? Paper presented at the Australian Association for Research in Education annual conference, Melbourne, December 2004

Walker, M. and Nixon, J. (eds) (2004) *Reclaiming Universities from a Runaway World*. Maidenhead: SRHE/Open University Press

Walker, M. (2006) 'First generation' students in England: social class narratives of university access and participation, *Theory and Research in Education*, forthcoming

Walkerdine, V., Lucey, H., and Melody, J. (2001) *Growing Up Girl: Psychosocial Explorations of Gender and Class*. Houndmills: Palgrave

Ward, L. (2004) UK degrees boost pay by 59%, *Education Guardian*, 15 September 2004

Watts, M. and Bridges, D. (2003) Accessing Higher Education: what injustice does the current widening participation agenda seek to transform? Paper presented to the Transforming Unjust Structures, capabilities and justice, Von Hugel Institute, St Edmunds College, Cambridge, June 2003

Wedekind, V. R (2001) A Figurational Analysis of the Lives and Careers of Some South African Teachers. Unpublished doctoral thesis, Faculty of Social Science and Law University of Manchester

Weiler, K. (1988) *Women teaching for change: Gender, class and power*. New York: Bergin and Garvey

Wilkinson, J. (2001) Designing a New Course; in M. Walker (ed.) (2001) *Reconstructing Professionalism in University Teaching*. Buckingham: SRHE/Open University Press

Winch, C. (2004) Developing Critical Rationality as a Pedagogical Aim, *Journal of Philosophy of Education*, 38(3): 467–84

Woodhall, M. (2001) Human capital: educational aspects; in N.J. Smelser and P.B. Baltes (eds) *International Encyclopaedia of the Social and Behavioral Sciences*, 10. Oxford: Elsevier

Wynn, J. (2004) Youth Transitions to Work and Further Education in Australia. Paper presented to the annual meeting of the American Educational Research Association, San Diego, April 2004

Young, I.M. (1990) *Justice and the politics of difference*. Princeton, NJ: Princeton University Press

Young, I.M. (2000) *Inclusion and Democracy*. Oxford: Oxford University Press

Zipin, L. and Brennan, M. (2004) Managerial Governmentality and the Suppression of Ethics; in Walker, M. and Nixon, J. (eds) (2004) *Reclaiming Universities from a Runaway World*. Maidenhead: SRHE/Open University Press

Index

The Society for Research into Higher Education

The Society for Research into Higher Education (SRHE), an international body, exists to stimulate and coordinate research into all aspects of higher education. It aims to improve the quality of higher education through the encouragement of debate and publication on issues of policy, on the organization and management of higher education institutions, and on the curriculum, teaching and learning methods.

The Society is entirely independent and receives no subsidies, although individual events often receive sponsorship from business or industry. The Society is financed through corporate and individual subscriptions and has members from many parts of the world. It is an NGO of UNESCO.

Under the imprint *SRHE & Open University Press*, the Society is a specialist publisher of research, having over 80 titles in print. In addition to *SRHE News*, the Society's newsletter, the Society publishes three journals: *Studies in Higher Education* (three issues a year), *Higher Education Quarterly* and *Research into Higher Education Abstracts* (three issues a year).

The Society runs frequent conferences, consultations, seminars and other events. The annual conference in December is organized at and with a higher education institution. There are a growing number of networks which focus on particular areas of interest, including:

Access	FE/HE
Assessment	Graduate Employment
Consultants	New Technology for Learning
Curriculum Development	Postgraduate Issues
Eastern European	Quantitative Studies
Educational Development Research	Student Development

Benefits to members

Individual

- The opportunity to participate in the Society's networks
- Reduced rates for the annual conferences
- Free copies of *Research into Higher Education Abstracts*
- Reduced rates for *Studies in Higher Education*

- Reduced rates for *Higher Education Quarterly*
- Free online access to *Register of Members' Research Interests* – includes valuable reference material on research being pursued by the Society's members
- Free copy of occasional in-house publications, e.g. *The Thirtieth Anniversary Seminars Presented by the Vice-Presidents*
- Free copies of *SRHE News* and *International News* which inform members of the Society's activities and provides a calendar of events, with additional material provided in regular mailings
- A 35 per cent discount on all SRHE/Open University Press books
- The opportunity for you to apply for the annual research grants
- Inclusion of your research in the *Register of Members' Research Interests*

Corporate

- Reduced rates for the annual conference
- The opportunity for members of the Institution to attend SRHE's network events at reduced rates
- Free copies of *Research into Higher Education Abstracts*
- Free copies of *Studies in Higher Education*
- Free online access to *Register of Members' Research Interests* – includes valuable reference material on research being pursued by the Society's members
- Free copy of occasional in-house publications
- Free copies of *SRHE News* and *International News*
- A 35 per cent discount on all SRHE/Open University Press books
- The opportunity for members of the Institution to submit applications for the Society's research grants
- The opportunity to work with the Society and co-host conferences
- The opportunity to include in the *Register of Members' Research Interests* your Institution's research into aspects of higher education

Membership details: SRHE, 76 Portland Place, London W1B 1NT, UK Tel: 020 7637 2766. Fax: 020 7637 2781. email: srheoffice@srhe.ac.uk world wide web: http://www.srhe.ac.uk./srhe/ *Catalogue*: SRHE & Open University Press, McGraw-Hill Education, McGraw-Hill House, Shoppenhangers Road, Maidenhead, Berkshire SL6 2QL. Tel: 01628 502500. Fax: 01628 770224. email: enquiries@openup.co.uk – web: www.openup.co.uk